Pardon My French

CHARLES TIMONEY

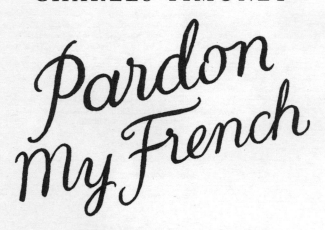

Pardon My French

Unleash Your Inner Gaul

PENGUIN BOOKS

PENGUIN BOOKS

Published by the Penguin Group
Penguin Books Ltd, 80 Strand, London WC2R ORL, England
Penguin Group (USA) Inc., 375 Hudson Street, New York, New York 10014, USA
Penguin Group (Canada), 90 Eglinton Avenue East, Suite 700, Toronto, Ontario, Canada M4P 2Y3
(a division of Pearson Penguin Canada Inc.)
Penguin Ireland, 25 St Stephen's Green, Dublin 2, Ireland (a division of Penguin Books Ltd)
Penguin Group (Australia), 250 Camberwell Road, Camberwell, Victoria 3124, Australia
(a division of Pearson Australia Group Pty Ltd)
Penguin Books India Pvt Ltd, 11 Community Centre, Panchsheel Park, New Delhi – 110 017, India
Penguin Group (NZ), 67 Apollo Drive, Rosedale, North Shore 0632, New Zealand
(a division of Pearson New Zealand Ltd)
Penguin Books (South Africa) (Pty) Ltd, 24 Sturdee Avenue, Rosebank,
Johannesburg 2196, South Africa

Penguin Books Ltd, Registered Offices: 80 Strand, London WC2R ORL, England

www.penguin.com

First published 2007
1

Set in 9.25/12.5 pt PostScript Linotype Sabon
Typeset by Rowland Phototypesetting Ltd, Bury St Edmunds, Suffolk
Printed in England by Clays Ltd, St Ives plc

ISBN: 978-1-846-14052-5

For Inès, Sarah and Sebastian

Into the face of the young man who sat on the terrace of the Hotel Magnique at Cannes there had crept a look of furtive shame, the shifty, hangdog look which announces that an Englishman is about to talk French.

The Luck of the Bodkins, P. G. Wodehouse

Contents

Acknowledgements   xi
Introduction   xiii

Food and Drink   1
The Country, and how to Get about It   27
Education   49
Entertainment and Sport   65
Paperwork   79
The Calendar Year   95
How to Sound French   109
Historical Matters and Perfidious Albion   141
Young People (and Their Slang)   153
Relations (Family and Others)   173
Day-to-day Life   191
The Business World   211

Index   227

Acknowledgements

We will see in the Introduction that I didn't know any of these words when I first came to France: a variety of longsuffering people had to teach them to me. So spare a thought for my first colleagues, those poor people who hadn't asked to have 'un Anglais' in their midst but who, thankfully for me, felt that 'un Anglais' who could speak a bit of French would be easier to have around than one who couldn't. So 'un grand merci' goes to Jean, Roland and Gaby at SBB, who did the groundwork in my spoken French as well as starting me on the dreadful stuff that you have to use in patents. Later on François and Marc at Elf took over and explained the subtleties and, among other things, put me off 'par contre' for life. Away from the office someone had to teach me the slang and all the other words you need to survive 'chez la belle famille'. For this, thanks go to Inès, Anne, Marc, Valérie, Nathalie and Eric.

On a more practical note, I would like to thank Jane Turnbull and Georgina Laycock, without whom I would have had to keep all these words to myself, and to Bela Cunha for tidying them all up.

Introduction

Some twenty years ago, my wife and I were both made redundant in the same month, an event that I perceived as disastrous but which she claimed was a sign that we should go and live for a while in her native France. So, in a moment of weakness, I agreed to apply for a job in Paris. The idea, at least for me, was to spend just a year or so there as an adventure in the hope that it would look good on my CV.

Having got the job (the fact that I was the only candidate may well have been a contributing factor), the main problem I was faced with over the first months was a staggering lack of useful French vocabulary. While the work that I did was in English, I obviously needed to talk to my colleagues, and deal with day-to-day living, in French. I had studied the language to O Level but it became frighteningly clear from the very first morning at work that this was far from enough. My colleagues consistently used a wide variety of impenetrable slang and persisted in the annoying habit of talking about things I had never heard of.

Conversations tended to go too fast for me to be able to ask for explanations so I spent most of the early months in France in a painful haze of incomprehension. I am convinced that I would have been able to follow at least some of what was going on if only I had known one or two key words. Surely, if you understand that people are talking about second-hand cars, or income tax, or even gift wrap, you will have more chance of keeping up.

It seems likely that many English visitors who spend time in France must have the same sort of experience. So, in order to give you, whatever your level of French, a better chance of following what people are talking about, making sense of what you see in the street, or even enabling you to leaf through a French newspaper and triumphantly think 'Oh! I've heard of that!', I have made a selection of the various words that would certainly have made my life a lot easier had I known them when I first started work here all those years ago.

The words have been chosen to be as useful as possible and to give you a broad understanding of French life: they are probably not words that you learned at school, nor are the definitions the sort of thing you find in most dictionaries.

I have grouped them by themes such as Food, Travel, Entertainment and the like. Even if you don't manage to remember them all, the explanations should provide a useful insight into what is really what in France.

Food and Drink

Where else could one start but with food and drink? One of the main reasons why so many people come on holiday to France is to take full advantage of its bars and restaurants.

But are you sure that you are ordering the right thing when you stop for a drink in a café? Are you getting the best value from your 'boulanger'? Why should you beware if a Frenchman wants to interest you in his chocolate bar? And what would you think if someone appeared to be asking you for a duck?

You will also discover a variety of French dishes, find reassurance about horses and get some useful advice about tipping.

DRINKS AND CAFÉS

Apéro *Apéro* is the familiar form of the word 'apéritif' and is definitely an important one to learn early on. With luck, you can encounter 'un *apéro*' either at the office or at home. At work, people treat their colleagues to an aperitif before a meal to celebrate the birth of a baby, or buying a new car, or to announce a change of job. I have fond memories of sitting down for lunch with colleagues, whereupon one would rub his hands together with delight and cry, 'Allez! C'est moi qui vous offre l'*apéro* aujourd'hui!' before going on to announce some especially good news. We also had a system whereby, if you lost a bet, you had to pay for the *apéros* for everyone. You can of course have aperitifs away from the office, whether before a meal at home with friends or at a restaurant. Inviting someone for an *apéro* or, more correctly, inviting them to 'venir prendre l'apéritif' is a pleasant and simpler alternative to inviting them to supper. Depending on how much food is served, an aperitif can last anywhere from an hour to all evening. The key element of decent *apéros* is good sparkling wine, preferably champagne, in generous quantities. The ultimate *apéro*, which can rival a meal, is something called an 'apéritif dinatoire'. If you get invited to such an *apéro* you can expect the drinks to be accompanied by several types of hot food and there should even be something sweet at the end.

Bière On one of my first forays into a pub with friends at the tender age of sixteen, my friend Paul called for 'Half a pint of beer, please.' This was met with hoots of derision from the landlord as, of course, in the UK you have to specify which sort of beer – bitter, brown ale, mild, etc. – you want. For once, things in France are simpler. You can go into a French bar and order 'Une *bière*, s'il vous plaît' without running the risk of being humiliated. The barman or waiter will generally ask for details, suggesting 'une pression', which means draught beer, or naming a few bottled beers for you to choose from. Experience teaches you that the list tends to start with the cheapest and work upwards. You can speed things up by calling at the outset for 'un demi', which will lead to the barman giving you a glass of draught beer straight away. 'Un demi' used to mean half a litre but now refers to 25cc or a quarter of a litre. Occasionally, you still hear older men in bars calling for 'un bock' when they don't want to drink a whole 'demi'. 'Un bock' is a wineglassful of beer, roughly half the quantity of a 'demi'. I don't know anyone who drinks 'bocks' as there is barely enough for a single swallow.

Canard First of all, you should never offer a French person granulated sugar with their coffee. If they are very polite, they will be visibly shocked; if they are not, they will react as though you are trying to poison them. Only sugar lumps should ever be offered with coffee. Having established this, you have discovered yet another of the many excellent reasons for going to France: dunking sugar lumps in coffee is absolutely divine. Dunking a sugar lump, preferably a large, oblong one, in a cup of strong black coffee is known as 'faire un *canard*' ('*canard*', as you know, usually means duck). When a group of people are together having coffee, it is quite common for a person who hasn't ordered one to pick up a sugar lump, lean over towards someone else's and ask, 'Je peux faire un *canard*?' They thus get a kick of sugary caffeine without having to drink a whole cup.

Champagne *Champagne* is sufficiently important in France to merit two special verbs to cover opening it and drinking it. For a start, you don't just say, 'On va boire du *champagne*,' because it would make it sound about as festive as drinking tap water. When people mean drinking generous quantities of *champagne*, they use the verb 'sabler' as, for example, 'Ce soir, on va sabler le *champagne*.' 'Sabler' doesn't mean open nor yet just drink; it means to drink a good lot of champagne on a festive occasion. There is also a really good word for opening a bottle of *champagne*. This is 'sabrer'. Even though the words look similar, they are quite different. 'Sabrer' literally means to cut with a sabre. Thus 'sabrer le *champagne*' means to whack the neck of the bottle with a sabre and so dispense with all that fiddling with the twisted wires. It is still used, even when no one is intending to get out their sword. The term apparently dates from one of the occupations of France by the Germans in the nineteenth century. Invading troops found themselves in the Champagne region and seem to have put their cavalry sabres to good use when liberating the contents of various cellars.

Coca The manufacturers of Coca-Cola apparently pride themselves that their product is the only one on the planet that has two world-famous names for it: Coca-Cola and Coke. In fact, they have reason to feel even more proud because the common word for their product in France is neither Coca-Cola nor Coke but simply *Coca*. Going into a French bar and ordering 'un Coke' will generally result in the barman repeating the order but with the words 'un *Coca*'. Ordering 'un *Coca*' – provided that's what you want! – is a good way of showing that you are starting to get the hang of things.

Coup This word literally means a blow or a knock and this explains why the first time someone offered me one in a bar, I took a quick step backwards. In fact, 'un *coup* à boire' is a drink. When you suggest going for a drink to someone you might say, 'Je t'offre un *coup* à boire?', or possibly 'Je te paie un *coup*?', which is somewhat less chic. (As a general rule, when treating someone to something, it is preferable to use 'offrir' rather than 'payer'.) Encouraging someone to come for a drink might involve saying, 'Allez! On va boire un *coup*?' and heading off purposefully towards the bar. As far as I can tell, *coup* applies only to alcoholic drinks; offering someone a soft drink would be phrased differently, for example, 'Tu veux boire quelque chose?' You can specify that the drink in question is red or white wine simply by adding on the appropriate colour. A glass of red wine is 'un *coup* de rouge', but calling it that does not say much for the quality of wine on offer. Finally, if you overdo your consumption of *coups* you are said to have 'bu un *coup* en trop' or more colourfully 'avoir un *coup* dans le nez'.

Deux . . . deux If you listen carefully the next time you go to a café or a brasserie, you will hear the double coffee order. Assuming it is not the sort of place where the waiter himself makes the coffee, he will call the order to the barman who will then get it ready and set the cups on the bar. What is interesting is that the waiter repeats the number of coffees ordered just after the word 'cafés'. Thus, instead of calling out, 'Deux cafés!', the waiter in fact shouts, '*Deux* cafés . . . *deux*!' This is presumably intended to give the barman a second or so to jerk himself from his reverie and think, 'What? Did someone call for coffee? But how many did he want?', whereupon he hears the second 'deux' right on cue. Some waiters do the double order for any drinks, shouting out, 'Trois Ricards . . . trois!' This seems to work only for orders of a single sort of drink. Composite orders like '*deux* pressions . . . *deux*, et un Ricard' would sound silly.

Eau de source Knowing about this earlier would have saved us money. Arriving in France, one of the first things you become aware of is the French obsession with mineral water. Plastic bottles of all shapes and sizes feature strongly on tables and desks across the land. At first sight, all the bottles have famous labels – Évian, Vittel, Volvic and Contrex being the most popular. These actually all taste different, the easiest to spot being Contrex, which tastes more strongly of minerals than any of the others. Such branded mineral waters are, however, surprisingly expensive, even when bought in bulk. Then came the happy day when we discovered that a basically similar product existed which sold at a fraction of the cost of the famous brands. This is generically labelled spring water or *eau de source*. Spring water comes in plain, cheap, litre-and-a-half bottles, or can be bought even more cheaply in huge plastic containers which hold several litres. The only problem with these is getting them home. At least lifting them up to pour the water is not a problem as they have a handy tap on the bottom. There used to be (and perhaps there still is) a spot in rue de la Pompe in Paris where spring water was available from a public tap. You would see people queuing with loads of empty mineral water bottles waiting to fill them up for free.

Pot A drinks party at work to celebrate a wedding, a birth or some other happy domestic event is commonly known as 'un *pot*'. People also do 'un *pot*' on their last day at work before retiring or before leaving for a new job. When you learn that a colleague has handed in his notice, is about to get married or has just produced an heir, someone will invariably ask, 'Quand est-ce qu'il fait son *pot*?', sure in the knowledge that a *pot* will be organized. In the days preceeding the *pot*, a collection goes round for a present, a procedure known as 'faire passer une enveloppe'.

Pourboire The French word for tip, which I include because any visitor to France should be aware that in French restaurants and bars, the tip is already included. In the old days, when you called for the bill, the waitress would add up all the things that you had ordered and then, in the blink of an eye, add on 15 per cent service charge. Now the price of each item shown on a menu already includes the tip. If you look at the bottom of a menu, it should say, in extremely small print, 'Service 15% inclus' or some such. Hard as it may be to believe, I have seen menus in tourist restaurants where this phrase has been inadvertently mistranslated as 'Service not included'. How they came to make a mistake like that is beyond me! In bars, if the barman or the waiter has been friendly, it is customary to leave a few centimes, despite the fact that you have in fact already tipped. The only problem with the tip being included – and at 15 per cent it can be a sizeable sum – is that you can't get out of paying it even if the service or the food has been awful. In the old days, if things were not satisfactory, you would simply not leave a tip at all. It is not clear whether the enforced inclusion of the service charge has led to better or worse service in restaurants and bars.

Zinc *Zinc* can be used to refer to a bar or to an aircraft, and in either sense should be pronounced more like 'zaing' than *zinc*.

Before the bars of French bistrots came to be covered in tiles, synthetic materials or imitation marble, the counter was made out of a sheet of zinc. Over the years, the metal surface became scratched and battered, giving the top of the bar a wonderful silvery patina. People would describe having had a drink 'sur le *zinc*' rather than 'au comptoir', an expression which is still common, even though zinc-topped bars no longer are.

BREAD AND CAKES

Baguette Of course you know what this is, and so did I when I first arrived in France. What I didn't know was that you don't have to buy the whole thing. Buying a whole *baguette* and then not eating all of it in the course of the day, used to annoy me intensely because the bread was stale by the next morning. Until the day when I heard someone ask for 'une demi-*baguette*' at my local BOULANGERIE. Half a *baguette* was handed over without a raised eyebrow. Indeed, I now realize that quite a few people, especially single people, regularly buy only half. You can even buy two halves in the course of one day and thus enjoy fresh bread both for breakfast and in the evening. There is more: experts who particularly like a crusty, or a less crusty, *baguette* go on to request one that is 'bien cuite' – well done – or 'pas trop cuite' – not too crusty. Another unexpected variant is offered by asking for something called 'une *baguette* moulée'. This is a loaf which has been baked in a shaped baking tray, rather than on a flat plate, and thus has a lower half that is softer and less crusty. All this should enable you to broaden your bread-buying horizons enormously.

Boulangerie/pâtisserie Setting off to buy bread in France can leave you with a choice between two shops, both apparently selling bread, but one labelled *Boulangerie*, while the other has a sign saying *Pâtisserie*. What is the difference? And which one should you choose? 'Une *boulangerie*' is a baker's shop. In it you should expect to find various types of bread, assorted PAINS AU CHOCOLAT, croissants and the like, collectively known as 'viennoiseries', and also a few nice cakes, which will probably be displayed in the shop window. 'Une *pâtisserie*' is an up-market *boulangerie*. It will have a similar range of breads and 'viennoiseries' but will offer a far broader choice of delicious cakes of all shapes and sizes, some of which will be very expensive indeed. If you just want bread, or are on a limited budget, it is probably a good idea to opt for a *boulangerie* so that you won't be tempted by the amazing cakes in the *pâtisserie*. This is especially good advice at the weekend when there are queues of people waiting for their cakes and 'tartes' to be wrapped up. Some bakers who are particularly proud of their bread-making will label themselves '*boulangerie* artisanale'. An 'artisan' is a craftsman.

Et avec ceci? This is the cry of bakers, greengrocers and butchers or any stallholder in a French market. You ask for your BAGUETTE, or a dozen spicy sausages called merguez, or a kilo of potatoes and the seller, once he has handed you your order, nicely wrapped up, will enquire, '*Et avec ceci?*' The question literally means And with this . . . ? and is intended to check whether you need anything else. Even if you have already asked for everything you want, the question has a secondary, and more important, function: to encourage you to look at the various wares before you and spot something you hadn't planned on buying. And so increase the value of the sale. Nine times out of ten you have no further purchase to make and thus will reply firmly, 'Ça sera tout, merci' – that will be all, thanks. Oddly enough, while the salesperson will have greeted you, and possibly checked some aspect of your order, in a perfectly normal voice, the all-important question '*Et avec ceci . . . ?*' will invariably be asked in a completely different, and generally irritating and ingratiating, tone. The whiny, subservient tone annoys me so much that I will reply, 'Ça sera tout, merci' even if I have actually thought of something else I need. Those unfamiliar with the question have been known to misunderstand it entirely, notably one local English resident who was asked it each time he went to the butcher's. He thought he was being asked 'Et avec saucisses?', and assumed that the butcher was enquiring whether he also wanted some sausages. His reply of 'Non merci, je n'en veux pas' must have been perplexing to the poor chap.

Gâteau A word that has caused me great disappointment over the years. The problem arose because I was taught it was the French for cake – a birthday cake, for example, being 'un *gâteau* d'anniversaire'. Came the first time at a friend's house that we were asked 'Vous voulez des *gâteaux*?' Images arose of chocolate cake, or some delicious fruit affair stuffed with cream. I accepted enthusiastically, only to see my host return with a plate of plain biscuits. It seems that *gâteaux* is a synonym for biscuits, the words being apparently interchangeable. If you are faced with an offer of a *gâteau*, the only clues you will have to work out what this means is that either it will be in the plural – 'des *gâteaux*' – in which case it is unlikely that there will be several cakes on offer, or they will be specified as being 'des petits *gâteaux*'. Were real cakes being offered, then small ones would be referred to as 'pâtisseries' and not 'petits *gâteaux*'. Old-fashioned, hard biscuits are generally called '*gâteaux* secs'. Obviously, if something is being referred to as 'sec' – dry – it is a good indication that it will not be a rich chocolate cake. There are also salty nibbles that are served with an APÉRO and are called '*gâteaux* apéritifs' or '*gâteaux* salés'. You really have to be on your guard whenever the word *gâteau* crops up in order to avoid being as disappointed as I was!

Pain au chocolat/chocolatine This is an example of something whose name changes according to where in France you order it. In Paris and in most of northern France, the delicious, flaky, buttery pastry roll with a length of chocolate inside it which revives you, in time of need, at any hour of the day, is known as a *pain au chocolat*. Once you head south and get below about the level of Bordeaux, if you go into a local baker and call for a *pain au chocolat*, you will be met with incomprehension. In the south, it is called a *chocolatine*. I have been known, when on holiday, to rush into the first bakery I see and order one, merely for the joy of using the word. Asking for a *chocolatine* in northern France will, of course, be met with similar incomprehension. If you get lost on the way to the south of France, and want to work out roughly where you are, ordering a *pain au chocolat* may be a means of finding out how far south you have actually travelled.

Tartine The French have two words for bread-based snack foods. One is SANDWICH, the other is *tartine*, which describes a single piece of bread on which is laid or spread whatever you fancy. *Tartines* do not necessarily have to have anything other than butter on them. Indeed, the ideal accompaniment to a cup of coffee in a bar early in the morning is 'une *tartine* beurrée' or two. This is a

piece of BAGUETTE, cut lengthways and generously buttered. Dipped into your coffee, it becomes quite simply delicious. You can have *tartines* with jam or cheese, or anything else you want. If the bread you have is a bit stale, you can grill it and make a '*tartine grillée*'.

FOOD AND MEALS

À cheval The sight of an item on a brasserie menu called 'hamburger avec oeuf *à cheval*' can lead to problems. In a country that is known for eating horses, the unwary may assume that the hamburger is made from horsemeat. I once witnessed an English family in a café, faced with such an item on the menu. After several minutes of loud, dark muttering, they were preparing to leave, until I stopped them by pointing out that '*à cheval*' translates as on horseback and simply means that your hamburger is topped with a fried egg. Should a dish on a menu contain horsemeat – which is extremely unlikely – this would be specified as being 'viande chevaline'. In the equally unlikely event that you actually want to buy horsemeat – and shame on you if you do – you should go to a specialized butcher's known as 'une boucherie chevaline'. They are easy to spot, and to avoid, as they usually have a sign with a horse's head outside the shop.

Bouffer We will see in the final section that people do not work in France. You will be equally surprised to learn that a lot of them don't seem to eat either. Rather than the word 'manger', many people use the familiar term *bouffer* when they talk about eating. Referring to consuming food as *bouffer*, however, makes it clear that what is being consumed is not expensive food of high quality – no one goes to La Tour d'Argent to *bouffer*! – but rather generous portions of good, wholesome stuff. After a big meal, one might exclaim, 'C'est fou ce qu'on a bouffé!', while children encourage family members to come and sit up by crying 'À table – on bouffe!' It is a good word to use if you are annoyed about someone eating all the chocolate – 'Qui a bouffé tout le chocolat?' There is a corresponding slang word for food which is 'bouffe'.

Café gourmand This is quite a recent invention which you come across mainly in steak houses or fish restaurants that are part of a chain. You have enjoyed your 'entrée + plat' and you don't have enough room for a huge pudding, but you really fancy something sweet, and preferably chocolaty. To cater for this, restaurants came up with the brilliant idea of a *café gourmand*. The word 'gourmand' doesn't relate to the coffee itself – that will be the regular, small black espresso. The 'gourmand' bit is what comes with it. What arrives is an artistic array of a cup of coffee and a selection of miniature puddings. You usually get three: a mini triangle of brownie, an eggcup-sized crème brûlée and a taste of something like 'clafoutis'. If you are having supper and don't want to be kept awake, you can always ask for a 'déca gourmand' where 'déca' is short for 'décaféiné'.

Couscous, cassoulet, choucroute, confit In the course of the first few months that I spent in France I discovered several new culinary delights, all of which begin with the letter C. The first, and still my favourite, was *couscous*. As I'm sure you know, couscous is the name for ground buckwheat, which is the base of this dish. The other ingredients are vegetables – which can include carrots, chick peas, courgettes, celery or parsnips; meat – a mix of lamb, either in the form of chops or kebabs, chicken or merguez; and a spicy paste called harissa. First you make a pile of ground buckwheat in the middle of your plate or bowl. Then mix some harissa (according to how hot you like your *couscous*) into some of the stock from the vegetables and pour it over the ground buckwheat. Some people like their *couscous* fairly dry; I like mine awash. Next, scoop on a good quantity of vegetables, pile your chosen bits of meat on top and you're ready.

After discovering *couscous* I went on to encounter *cassoulet*, which is a far heavier affair. It comes originally from either Toulouse or Castelnaudary, depending on which cookery book you believe, and is a dish based on white beans cooked in a tomato sauce and mixed with chunks of meat and sausage. It is great on winter evenings but is not recommended for those watching their waistlines.

Then there's *choucroute*, which comes typically from the Alsace region of eastern France. *Choucroute* is pickled cabbage, cooked in white wine – which is far nicer than you might imagine – served with boiled potatoes, chunks of pork, sausages, slices of ham and lots of mustard. You should really wash it down with loads of beer, but you can drink white wine instead, if you prefer.

The final C that I encountered was *confit*. '*Confit* de canard' is a gastronomic delight. Portions of cooked duck are preserved in a jar or a tin in large quantities of duck fat. You then heat up the duck – whether under the grill or in the oven – fry potatoes in the fat, and accompany the lot with a red wine from the south-west such as Madiran. This is quite simply paradise!

Crème anglaise I put this in because it contains the word 'anglaise' and you might feel bound to order it, if you spotted it on a menu, simply out of patriotism. *Crème anglaise* means custard. Calling it that though just doesn't do it justice. It is custard revised and corrected. It is custard as it should truly be, or custard as it would have been if some other country had invented it. Come to think of it, that is just what the French did. *Crème anglaise* is more liquid, tastes more of vanilla and is simply smoother and more sophisticated-looking than custard, especially when the custard is made from powder out of a tin (even though I used to really enjoy mixing up the paste when I was small). All sorts of delicious French puddings, including such wonders as 'gâteau au chocolat amer', come with a serving of *crème anglaise*. You spoon it over your pudding and watch it run down the sides. And it tastes delicious!

Cuisson You have just ordered a reviving steak in a restaurant but, before the waiter sets off to tell the kitchen he will enquire, 'Et la *cuisson*?' How do you want it cooked? There are four basic degrees of cooking that you can ask for. The first is 'bleu' or blue. It may well be called that because the meat is blue with cold as it certainly won't have been cooked, it's merely been seared briefly on both sides. Seeing a 'steak bleu' for the first time, you may get the impression that it has just been shown to the cook before being brought to your table. It is an acquired taste, much like steak tartare. The next step up is 'saignant' – bloody. This corresponds to rare and means that the meat has actually been cooked rather than just left beside the cooker. Purists believe that the best way to enjoy a steak is 'saignant'. If that's what they like, fine. Then we come to 'à point' which is medium rare. This is considered the normal degree of cooking by many people, including most tourists.

Things get tricky if you want to have your steak well done. You have two choices: either you go to a tourist eatery where they don't care what you make them do to a steak, or you go to a proper restaurant and boldly ask for your steak 'bien cuit'. If it is a steak restaurant, there is a fair chance that you are going to have to fight at this point. The waiter, proud in his role of self-appointed steak expert, will not take kindly to someone asking for a steak that he considers to be overdone. I have heard steak house waiters tell customers that if they want their steak 'bien cuit' they can go and eat it somewhere else. If you don't feel up to the hassle you can take the easy option and order your steak 'à point' and then drink lots of wine before it arrives.

This cooking inquisition can also apply to other cuts of meat, for example 'magret de canard'.

Eau When ordering food in a restaurant, there comes a tricky moment when the waiter will quizz you about your water requirements. He will typically start off by casually suggesting that you might like some water, and you may well agree that this would be a good idea. Then, if you don't beat him to it, he will ask something like, '*Eau* plate ou gazeuse?' At this point, it is not too late to choose, not simply between still and fizzy water, but between those two and free tap water. All French restaurants are prepared to serve you a jug of water should you ask for one. They would, of course, much rather sell you a nice bottle of mineral water. But if mineral water is what you generally drink, then why not? If you want a particular brand name, for example Vittel, you can order 'une Vittel' rather than the more long-winded 'une bouteille de Vittel'. What's more, if you are thirsty, but don't want to get too drunk too quickly, you can call for a bottle of mineral water as an APÉRO.

You should, however, be warned that the more expensive the restaurant, the smaller the bottle, while the price, inversely, will be larger. If you don't want to invest in mineral water, you should act quickly before anyone starts mentioning it by calling for 'une carafe d'*eau*'. Don't worry, even if you have been beaten to it by the waiter, you can still firmly request one at a later stage, though you may find yourself having to insist a bit.

Formule This is a term that features on many menus, even in restaurants not intended for tourists. 'Une *formule*' is a fixed-price menu and can be expressed in a number of ways. *Formules* can be defined by price – 'notre *formule* à 15 euros' – or by name – 'notre *formule* rapide' or 'notre *formule* pêcheur' – or by the elements that make it up. In this last case, the *formule* will specify whether it relates to three courses – 'entrée, plat, dessert' – or to a choice between either 'entrée + plat' or 'plat + dessert'. When you are strolling past a number of restaurants reading the menus displayed outside, it is very easy to misread a *formule* and believe that you are going to get three courses, only to find out once you are sitting down inside that it's only a choice of two. Tourist restaurants tend to advertise for the sort of customers they are seeking by offering a '*formule* touristique'. This is something that could well make you carry on to the next restaurant.

Galette It is not so much the word *galette* that causes problems; rather it is the ritual that accompanies their consumption that takes a bit of getting used to. A *galette* or, more precisely, '*galette* des rois' is a round, flat, covered sweet tart which contains a layer of marzipan. It has nothing to do with the biscuits called '*galettes* bretonnes'. A '*galette* des rois' is served, preferably warm, on

Twelfth Night, 6 January, to celebrate the visit of the three kings to the infant Jesus. A typical *galette* contains a 'fève' (a dried broad bean) or a small ceramic figure of the baby Jesus. Whoever gets the 'fève' or the baby Jesus in their slice of *galette* becomes king and has to wear the golden cardboard crown that is usually included with the *galette* by the baker. As you can sometimes spot the 'fève' or the figurine once the *galette* has been cut into slices, the French have developed a system for sharing out the slices without any possible cheating. This ritual is followed both at home and, as I discovered to my astonishment, at work. Someone, often the youngest person in the group, is chosen by all those present to crawl under the table in the room where the *galette* is being eaten. As each slice is put on a plate ready to be handed out, the person under the table is asked to name who should receive it. This is done for all the slices, the person under the table awarding themselves one at some point during the ceremony. The oddest thing about this procedure is the fact that no one appears to find it odd at all, even when it is carried out in an office!

La Chandeleur There are two days on which the French traditionally eat pancakes. First of all, they are eaten, as they are in England, on Shrove Tuesday or Mardi Gras. But there is a second day for pancake consumption known as *La Chandeleur*. This falls on 2 February and is a Christian feast day that corresponds to Candelmas, the day of Christ's presentation at the temple. Mind you, hardly any French people know what *La Chandeleur* signifies other than that it is an excuse for excessive consumption of pancakes or crêpes. Apparently, it is to do with the coming of the end of winter and the return of sunlight. Not only are pancakes eaten on twice as many occasions as they are in England but the way in which they are eaten is different too. I was brought up to eat pancakes (on Shrove Tuesday but on no other date) with a squirt of lemon juice. Such an idea would never catch on with the sweet-toothed French. Here pancakes are typically eaten sprinkled with granulated sugar, preferably with a bit of fresh butter spread over them first. It beats lemon juice any day!

Manger chaud Food is important in France. The average French person will expect to eat meat at least once a day and will also expect at least one dish of each main meal to be served hot. Suggesting that a colleague might skip a decent meal and grab a sandwich may well be met with an appalled cry of 'Mais, il faut *manger chaud*!' or possibly 'Il faut *manger chaud* le midi' – see MIDI. *Manger chaud* is not exactly grammatically correct – 'chaud' is, after all, an adjective not an adverb. Nevertheless, eating a hot dish at mealtimes is sacred. We once stopped to buy wine at a vineyard in the wilds of France without realizing it was lunchtime. The lady of the house opened the door and promptly sent us packing, complaining that we had disturbed them at the most inconvenient of moments as 'On en est au chaud!' – we are at the hot course. It wasn't only that we had shown great insensitivity by dragging her from her cooked meal, what really upset the woman was that we were ringing doorbells at a time when we should quite obviously have been having our own hot meal somewhere.

Marrons *Marrons* are chestnuts, a food which seems to feature more often in the French diet than in the UK. No Christmas meal – see RÉVEILLON – would be complete without a dish of chestnuts, though I for one have never managed to show much enthusiasm for cooked chestnuts. 'Crème de *marrons*', on the other hand, is a delicious, sickly sweet substance which is absolutely wonderful when stirred into 'fromage blanc'. Wild chestnuts are known as 'châtaignes'. A French tradition in the autumn involves going to pick up 'châtaignes' in the forest and then roasting them over a log fire. Oddly enough, both *marron* and 'châtaigne' are slang words for a punch. In rugby matches, when the players get upset about something and start thumping each other, the commentator may describe the generous exchange of punches as 'une distribution de *marrons*'.

Monsieur

Clearly, this is not a food word, but it is a word that is often misused by British people in restaurants. On pleasant occasions when we have been out to eat with visiting friends, I have noticed that they can get carried away and become overly polite to the waiters. The problem stems from the fact that people tend to repeat what they hear. The waiter, addressing a male customer, will politely call him *Monsieur*. This is a quite right and proper thing for a well-brought-up waiter to do. Inexperienced foreign customers, however, try too hard to enter into the spirit of the thing and reply to the waiter by calling him *Monsieur* as well. This is silly. There is a kind of master–servant relationship between the two parties. While the waiter has to be subservient to the master, the master can't adopt the same deference in reply or the relationship breaks down. By all means, be polite to the waiter, but don't call him *Monsieur* when ordering. If you really want to, you can call him *Monsieur*! when trying to attract his attention. Some people do this, though most seem to just call 'S'il vous plaît!' in an interrogative way.

Incidentally, no one seems to call café waiters 'Garçon!' any more, even though 1950s French films encourage you to believe that you should.

Pain Bread at mealtimes is sacred in France. You only have to catch an evening commuter train to see lots of weary people clutching their BAGUETTES to eat with their supper. This means that in almost all French restaurants – we will come to the exceptions in a moment – bread will be provided free, and without you having to ask for it. You will soon realize that both the containers and the type of bread offered vary with the quality of the restaurant. The bread can come in a cheap, shiny metal basket, with or without a lining of paper napkin, or, if you move upmarket, it will be served in a rustic wicker basket with a pretty linen lining. The basic restaurant provides only diagonally sliced chunks of BAGUETTE. Spending more on your meal means that you can expect a selection of breads, both white and brown, even including the delicious 'Poilâne'. And what about butter? As far as I can see, you can expect to be given butter only in the most expensive places. But, wherever you go, if you finish the bread you have been given, you can always ask for more. The only places where you don't seem to get bread are Asian restaurants and crêperies.

Pêche I am sure that the French fondness for things gastronomic explains why so many fruit and vegetable words are commonly used to mean other things. For example, *pêche* means peach, but 'avoir la *pêche*' means to feel in really great shape. After your second cup of coffee at work, you might be heard to declare 'J'ai vraiment la *pêche* ce matin!' (Another expression for this is 'avoir la frite', whereas 'frites' usually means chips.) 'Poire' means pear but can also be a slang word for face, or can be used in the expression 'bonne poire' to mean idiot or sucker. People tend to call themselves 'bonne poire' after they have been forced into doing something unpleasant by someone with a strong personality. 'Pomme', meaning apple, forms part of the expression 'pauvre pomme', which also means idiot or sucker. 'Banane' is a children's insult for an idiot.

When it comes to vegetables, 'patate', which is a familiar word for potato, can also be used to mean idiot. You hear children calling to each other, 'Eh! Patate!'

Sandwich The first thing to note is that the French plural of *sandwich* is *sandwichs*. The second thing is that, when you order a *sandwich*, you get what you ask for. You can easily check this by ordering a ham *sandwich* in a bar. If you ask for 'un *sandwich* au jambon' you will get one, but there won't be any butter on the bread because you haven't asked for it. If you want ham and butter in your *sandwich*, you have to ask for 'un jambon beurre'. Doing this will mark you out as someone who knows about *sandwichs*, rather than some gormless idiot who stumblingly calls for 'un *sandwich* au jambon avec du beurre'. If you want a ham and cheese *sandwich*, you should ask for 'un mixte' or 'un jambon fromage' but, again, there won't be any butter. And if you fancy 'saucisson sec', then just ask for that. However, if you want to be cool and have butter too you could order 'un sec beurre', which will get you both 'saucisson' and butter for a minimum of effort.

Tablette de chocolat A splendid example of the different ways the Brits and the French view things! The Brits are very keen on drinking beer while the French are very keen on sweet things. A finely muscled male stomach, which in the UK is known as a six-pack, to a Frenchman brings to mind une *tablette de chocolat* or large bar of chocolate. This is strange since over-consumption of either beer or chocolate will make achieving such a stomach impossible.

Trou Normand This is a wonderful invention that can transform a heavy meal, leaving a feeling of well-being where there might otherwise have been indigestion. In certain restaurants (generally the more expensive ones), in the middle of a long and extravagant meal the waiter will arrive unexpectedly with a small glass or dish containing a refreshing mix of sorbet and alcohol. This is a *Trou Normand* and usually comprises apple or lemon sorbet swimming in a generous shot of Calvados. It doesn't always feature on the menu but simply appears at exactly the moment you are ready for it. Somehow, the mix of tangy sorbet and strong alcohol revives you from your food-and-drink-induced stupor and sets you up for the following courses.

Other regions have variants on the theme using different flavours of sorbet mixed with the local brandy or marc.

The Country, and how to Get about It

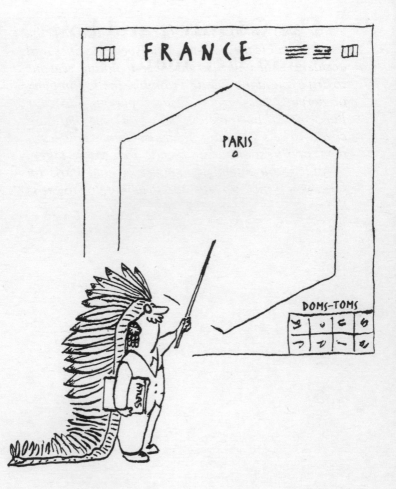

Those who go to France by car to discover the country will learn how to avoid speeding fines and accidents and will also discover tempting reasons to drive round the Arc de Triomphe in the company of nervous passengers. Visitors planning to tour Paris on public transport will find that there are cheap tickets available while everyone will learn what best to shout when having your photo taken.

And if you intend to wander around Paris on foot, you'll pick up tips about where not *to cross the road.*

ON THE ROAD

Appel de phares 'Faire un *appel de phares*' is to flash your headlights at someone. In the UK, you flash your lights if you are in a good mood and want to let someone out from a side road or allow them to turn right in front of you. You can also do it aggressively to show how cross you are about something, wishing that your lights were high-intensity lasers that would vaporize the offender and really teach them a lesson. While the French can flash their lights aggressively with the best of them, they are not used to lights being flashed kindly and rarely understand that you are letting them out (probably because the idea of letting someone out has never occurred to them). However, the major use of flashed headlights in France is to warn someone coming the other way that he is approaching a police speed camera. Any motorist worth his salt, if he spots a police car lurking by the roadside, or sees a radar trap, will flash the next two or three cars coming towards him to warn them of the impending danger. This shouldn't be seen as French generosity for the oncoming driver. Rather, it is simply a means of spoiling things for the policemen who are lying in wait. So, if you are driving along a main road in France and two or three consecutive cars flash their lights, slow down! By the way, flashing your lights to warn other drivers is actually illegal in France.

Bison Futé This means literally cunning bison and tends to conjure up images of a particularly astute Red Indian brave. It is the name chosen by the French national road traffic organization, whose job it is to keep people informed of roadworks and advise holidaymakers which days and times should be avoided when leaving or returning so as to try to lessen the congestion around the major cities. *Bison Futé* publish handy maps of secondary routes – known as 'Itinéraires bis' – that they recommend, for example, if you want to avoid a six-hour traffic jam north of Lyons. These routes are indicated by green arrows with 'Itinéraire bis' on them. *Bison Futé* also give news bulletins on the television before particularly busy weekends in which they advise drivers that the following Saturday will be a 'journée rouge', and travel should be avoided if at all possible. The only thing worse than a 'journée rouge' is a 'journée noire', which generally occurs only on the weekend of the August public holiday, when every car in France seems to be on the road. People take *Bison Futé*'s advice quite seriously and can be heard refusing invitations for a weekend in the country because '*Bison Futé* prévoit une journée rouge'.

Circulez! This is the traditional cry of a French traffic policeman to a motorist and is quite mystifying when you first hear it as, despite what you might imagine, there is no intention to make anyone drive in circles. It is related to the word 'circulation', which means traffic flow, where no rotation is involved either. When used by a policeman, '*Circulez!*' is just an instruction to keep on going or, if you are stationary, to start moving as soon as possible. If you have been stopped for some reason by a patrolman, you will most likely be dismissed at the end of the interview with a brisk '*Circulez!*' or, if you have irritated him, by a distinctly sharper '*Allez! Circulez!*' It is a good idea to get going as soon as possible at this point. People, whether on foot or in a car, who have stopped to gawp at an accident or other roadside drama, will be urged to stop

staring and move on with the words '*Circulez!* Il n'y a rien à voir!'
– Move along! There's nothing to see!

Clous The correct term for a pedestrian crossing is 'un passage
clouté' but everyone seems to just call them les *clous*. A pedestrian
crossing in the UK is intended to provide a safe place to cross the
road. It is clearly marked with Belisha beacons, broad white stripes
and silver studs, and UK motorists know that, when they see a
pedestrian waiting to cross the road, they should stop and let them
across. The grateful pedestrian will thank the motorist and it is all
wonderfully civilized and safe. Parisian pedestrian crossings look
disconcertingly like British ones. They don't have Belisha beacons
but they do have the same broad white stripes and lines of silver
studs, called *clous* or nails, clearly marking them. At first sight,
therefore, they look deceptively inviting. However, the principal
difference between the two nations' crossings is that, in France, the
clous and the stripes do not define a safe place to cross, they define
a target zone. In the unlikely event that a motorist spots someone
waiting to cross at a crossing, he will feel more entitled than ever
to try to run them over. In its way, it is all very civilized. Both
Parisian motorists and pedestrians know that, if you want to cross
the road, you do it elsewhere than on a crossing. By choosing a
spot picked at random, far away from a crossing, the pedestrian
will considerably increase their chances of survival. This means
that if you ever happen to spot a tourist trying to cross the Champs
Élysées on a crossing – the mere fact that he is embarked on such
a foolhardy attempt clearly marks him as a tourist – and you see a
car stop and let him across, your first reaction should be to check
the car's number plate. I can guarantee that it will be foreign.

Consommation Visitors to France not only have to learn a huge number of new words, they also have to learn new ways of looking at common problems. In the UK, the petrol consumption of a car is measured in miles per gallon. This is an easy term to visualize as the bigger the number, the more efficient your car and the less petrol you have to buy. France using litres instead of gallons and kilometres instead of miles, one might reasonably assume that petrol consumption would be measured in kilometres per litre. Not a bit of it. For reasons that I have never fathomed, in France your car's efficiency is measured in l/100 km or the number of litres it will use to travel 100 kilometres. Thus, the smaller the number of litres – eight or so – the better the consumption. In the UK, it is a relatively easy matter when you fill up at a petrol station to divide the number of miles you have driven by the number of gallons you bought and so get an idea of your mpg. In France, if you buy 44 litres of petrol after driving 625 kilometres, it requires considerable mental agility to work out your l/100 km figures. I'll leave you to find the answer to this example.

Constat The French like forms for things. A good example is a '*constat* à l'amiable', which is a jointly agreed accident report. This is a multi-coloured form that is to be found in the glove compartment of practically all French cars. In the event of an accident, the two parties (assuming that there are two) pull themselves from the wreckage, shout at each other for a while, and then the calmer of the two will get out his *constat*. The form has two columns setting out, in the manner of a multiple-choice questionnaire, various possible circumstances to describe what each party was doing at the time of the accident, e.g. pulling out without looking, backing on to a busy main road, or changing lanes to avoid a goat. Each party completes his column, adds a little drawing showing damage to each vehicle, and then retains a copy. This form is sent to the insurance company. It is common for people to fill in their car make and registration number, as well as their insurance policy details, before putting the form in the glove compartment. (Well, I do.) This makes the filling in of the form in the event of an accident a little bit easier. The French always express amazement that the British manage to have accidents and claim on their insurance without the benefit of an equivalent of a *constat*. I have never been able to explain to their satisfaction how we do.

Feux 'Les *feux*' is the familiar form for 'les *feux* de signalisation' or traffic lights. People tell you the way by saying things like 'Prenez à droite aux *feux*'. I include the word here, not because it is in any way tricky, but merely as an excuse to point out that French traffic lights do not go red; red and amber; green; amber; red, as they do in the UK. They miss out the stage of red and amber and leap directly from red to green, much in the manner of the start of a Formula 1 race. This perhaps explains the urgency with which many drivers set off from traffic lights, not to mention the split-second delay between the lights going green and the first hoot from the car behind you if you don't start moving fast enough.

Priorité à droite One of the reasons why driving in France is so memorable stems from the extraordinary French motoring rule known as *priorité à droite*. This states that, unless there is an indication to the contrary, where two roads of any size intersect, the vehicle arriving from the right has priority over the vehicle on the other road. At first glance this seems simple. In fact it is quite simply mad. What it means in practice is that if you are driving along even a main road, a person on a little side road coming in from the right (don't forget that people drive on the right here) can, unless there is a sign to the contrary, just drive straight out in front of you, causing you to slam on your brakes. If you are a careful sort and want to avoid sudden braking, you will tend to slow down at the first sight of a road joining from the right. You thus waste time and an incalculable amount of petrol, for absolutely nothing. *Priorité à droite* is also very important at roundabouts (see ROND POINT). You even hear tales of people driving slowly along a quiet road whereupon a car leaps out from a turning to the right and causes a crash, but where the decrepit state of that car suggests strongly that the accident has been caused on purpose so as to claim on the insurance of the person driving on the main road.

PV *PV* is short for 'procès-verbal', which, in its formal sense, is a written document intended to provide legally acceptable proof that an event took place. It can also mean the minutes of a formal meeting. In its more common form, however, it means a ticket, either for speeding or for a parking offence. When complaining about being given one, no one ever says 'J'ai eu un procès-verbal', they call it 'un *PV*'. Once you have landed yourself with a *PV*, you have two possible courses of action: if you are a person with no connections, you just grumble and pay up. If, however, you have friends or relatives who work in government or in the police force, you take full advantage of this by asking whoever it is to make your *PV* disappear. This practice, which appears infuriatingly unfair to those of us who don't know anyone useful, is known as 'faire sauter ses *PV*'. There is a rare third alternative which arises every five years at election time. Traditionally, the newly elected President will thank the electorate by declaring an amnesty of all parking

fines and those traffic violations which aren't considered too outrageous. I know colleagues who ignore final demands for payment
in the months preceding an election in the hope of such an amnesty.
You need nerves of steel!

Rond point Roundabouts all used to be based on the PRIORITÉ
À DROITE principle. Note the 'all used to be', it is important. This
principle meant that the person joining the roundabout had priority
over the person already on it. You could therefore hurtle on to any
roundabout with impunity, only to have to give way at the next
road coming in. The rule was illogical and many roundabouts have
since been changed to the UK system where the person on the
roundabout has priority over the one joining it. However, it is not
clear until you are very close to a roundabout in France whether it
is the old sort or the new sort. Indeed, many people still drive the
old way regardless of the true nature of the roundabout. It is, of
course, much more fun that way. The old rule still applies in many
places, most notably at Étoile in Paris, the roundabout around the
Arc de Triomphe. This is somewhere lunacy and anarchy apparently reign unchecked, but which in fact works according to strict
rules. It is thus a great place to take visitors. They will be appalled
by the apparent unchecked mayhem and will not have time to spot
the underlying rules, mainly because they will spend much of the
time with their eyes shut or hiding under their seat. There are twelve
streets joining Étoile, one every 30° or so. What makes the whole
thing so special is that you have priority coming on to the roundabout but you lose it just as soon as the next road comes in from
your right. If the traffic lights give you a good run-up towards
Étoile, you can hurtle into a maelstrom of moving cars in the happy
knowledge that everyone will have to slam on their brakes to keep

out of your way. Of course, the feeling of freedom is short-lived as you will have to slam on your own brakes shortly afterwards in order to let in people from the next avenue. This is a good thing because it gives you a perfect excuse to do some enthusiastic hooting and alarm your passengers still further.

PUBLIC TRANSPORT

Carnet You probably know all about this, but on my first visit to Paris many years ago, I resolutely bought Métro tickets one by one as and when I needed them. It seemed perfectly reasonable to do so – it's what you do in London. This was unfortunate as, being an impoverished student who was trying to see as much of Paris as possible on the cheap, I would have been delighted to learn that there was a more economical way to buy them. Bought singly, a Métro ticket currently costs €1.40. However, if you buy them ten at a time, you pay only €10.70. This works out at a considerable saving. A group of ten tickets is called 'un *carnet*'. *Carnet* literally means a notebook or book. When you buy 'un *carnet* de timbres' you get ten stamps in a little book. However, when you order 'un *carnet*' of Métro tickets you don't get a book, just ten individual tickets in a wad. RER tickets, as well as suburban train tickets, can also be bought more cheaply in *carnets*.

Carte orange A travel card for Parisian commuters is 'une *carte orange*'. As the name suggests, it is an orange-coloured card with the user's details and photo and comes wrapped in a plastic sleeve with a little pocket to hold the 'coupon', a plastic ticket the size of a Métro ticket that gives unlimited travel in a certain geographical zone of Paris for one month. Each month, people with a *carte orange* go to a Métro station and order 'un coupon mensuel deux zones' for example, and thus acquire another month's travel. Zones one and two cover central Paris, with zones three to six extending out into the suburbs. *Cartes oranges* are surprisingly reasonable, especially when compared to season ticket prices in the UK. What's more, most employers reimburse half the cost of the coupon each month. There is now a yearly travel card, also valid for a given geographical zone, which is called 'Navigo'. This is slightly cheaper than a year's worth of coupons and also avoids having to queue at the ticket office each month. Its other main advantage is that you just have to wave it over the ticket barrier rather than stop, take out your coupon and pass it through a reader.

Composter Much confusion arose the first time I saw signs at a railway station instructing me to *composter* something or other. In fact, it has nothing to do with gardening; *composter* means to punch your train ticket. At the end of each platform in any railway station you will find one or more orange pillars about four feet high. You simply slide the end of your ticket into a slot near the top of the pillar and you are rewarded by a loud stamping sound. Retrieving your ticket will reveal it to have a semi-circular hole punched along one edge and the date stamped at one end. You may be tempted not to *composter* your ticket in the hope of using it another time. This is not a good idea at all as checks are frequent and it is less likely nowadays that you can escape a fine by simply pretending to be a stupid English tourist. (Please excuse the tautology.) Before resorting to increased fines, the railway company tried to discourage people from catching trains without a ticket with a poster campaign based on the slogan 'Frauder: c'est bête' – Fare-dodging is stupid. This was rapidly withdrawn because most of the posters were defaced with the additional words 'mais payer, c'est encore plus bête' – but paying is even more stupid.

RATP, RER, SNCF Commuter travel in Paris is handled by three different mass transit companies. The Métro lines and all the Parisian buses are the responsibility of the *RATP* – Régie Autonome des Transports Parisiens – which was created in 1949. The fact that one company handles both means that a Métro ticket can also be used on a bus. This is practical because you can carry a CARNET with you to use on either means of transport. Métro lines, like bus routes, are known by a number, while the direction on the Métro is shown by the name of the terminus. The *RER* – Le Réseau Express Régional – looks after the suburban lines, each known by a letter rather than a number, which sweep across Paris from north to south and from one side to the other. *RER* trains are much bigger than Métro trains, go faster and are often double-deckers. As well as suburban *RER* lines, there are suburban railway lines, leading to the main railway stations. These are run by the *SNCF* – Société Nationale des Chemins de Fer – which is also responsible for the main, long-distance trains. Unless you have a CARTE ORANGE, you will need separate tickets for the *RER* and *SNCF* trains.

GEOGRAPHY

DOM-TOM The word 'colonie' was officially banished in 1945. The remains of the French empire are now known as 'les *DOM-TOM*', which stands for 'Départements d'Outre Mer' – or overseas counties – and 'Territoires d'Outre Mer' – or overseas territories. The French 'départements' or counties include five overseas ones, namely Guadeloupe (971), Martinique (972), Guyane (973), Réunion (974) and St Pierre et Miquelon (975). They are treated like the other French counties, even though they are rather a long way from all the others. They are generally shown on the handy little map that you get at the back of French diaries. The *TOM* are even further away and comprise Nouvelle Calédonie, Polynésie Française, Wallis et Futuna and les Terres Australes et Antarctiques Françaises. These are treated differently from the *DOM*, but are still subject to French laws.

Hexagone If you look at a map of France, close your eyes and let your imagination loose, you might think of the country as being roughly hexagonal. If you ignore the fact that the coasts and inland borders are far from straight, such a notion is not that far-fetched. A first side of the hexagon goes from the bottom of the Atlantic coast, down by Spain, and stretches up to Brest. The second carries on from Brest to the Belgian border. From there, the third side heads south-east down into Alsace. The fourth links Alsace to Monaco, while the fifth goes over to the start of the Pyrenees. The final side returns from there to the Atlantic coast at St-Jean-de-Luz. Having carried out this exercise in visualization, you may be wondering what the point of it all was. It was necessary in order to appreciate why on news and weather programmes the French quite often refer to their country as 'l'*hexagone*'.

Maghreb The old French empire included the *Maghreb*. This is the collective name for Algeria, Morocco and Tunisia. A native of any of these countries is commonly known as a 'Maghrébin'. There is also a common term relating to a native of Algeria, or, more precisely, from a particular mountainous region of Algeria, which is 'Kabyle'.

PARIS AND THE SUBURBS

Étoile Charles de Gaulle airport north of Paris and Place Charles de Gaulle, home to the Arc de Triomphe, have something in common: hardly anyone – except tourists, who don't count – refers to them by their proper name. No 'Parisien' would dream of getting into a taxi, or buying an RER train ticket, and asking for 'L'aéroport Charles de Gaulle, s'il vous plaît.' People call the place 'l'aéroport de Roissy' or more commonly just Roissy. Thus, when asked where they are flying from, people will reply, 'Je pars de Roissy.' Similarly, when the area around the Arc de Triomphe is referred to, it is known simply as 'l'Étoile', taxi drivers asking, 'On passe par l'Étoile?', while Métro passengers say things like 'Je vais descendre à l'Étoile' or 'Il faut changer à l'Étoile.' Some people try to compromise by calling it Place Charles de Gaulle-Étoile, but this is impossibly long-winded. All this should not lead you to believe that the late 'Grand Charles' is in any way unpopular. It is just that people find the original names easier and quicker to say.

Neuf trois – 93 The counties or 'départements' around Paris have numbers that go from 91 to 95, Paris itself being 75, as you know. These neighbouring 'départements' have completely different social characters, ranging from Les Hauts de Seine just to the west of Paris, which is by far the most chic – I used to live there – through L'Essonne to the south and Le Val de Marne to the east, neither of which is particularly remarkable. To the north-east, however, lies La Seine Saint-Denis, whose county number is 93. This should be referred to as 'quatre-vingt-treize', assuming that you ever have cause to talk about it. However, the residents of this 'département' enjoy such an unfavourable reputation in the eyes of Parisians that people have taken to calling it 'le *neuf trois*' instead. This is intended to show, somewhat cruelly, that inhabitants of 93 are so dim that they can't even pronounce the complicated number of their own county and are forced to call it by the individual figures instead. Anyone who is lucky enough to live elsewhere will refer to 'les habitants du *neuf trois*', making sure they pronounce it in as unflattering a way as possible. People like to note the number plates of cars – the last two figures show which county it comes from – and, when they spot a 93 driving badly, exclaim loudly, 'Ça m'étonne pas – c'est un *neuf trois*' – what do you expect from a 93.

Parigot The inhabitants of Paris, or those who were born there and still bear the hallmarks, are 'Parisiens'. This is often replaced by the slang term *parigot*, which can either refer to a person or be an adjective. A Parisian accent is thus 'un accent *parigot*'. But Parisians do not necessarily enjoy the best of reputations in the eyes of the inhabitants of the rest of France, and as French car number plates have the number of the county of origin as their last two figures, they can easily be spotted when away from their home city. Poor Parisian driving on holiday regularly leads to derisive cries from the locals of 'Eh! *Parigot*!' When circumstances demand stronger criticism, as they often do, angry locals may shout unflattering things such as '*Parigot* – tête de veau!'

Périphérique Paris had its original inner ring road years ago. It is known as 'les Boulevards des Maréchaux' because each section is known by the name of one of Napoleon's marshals. However, these boulevards are just ordinary roads and thus are festooned with traffic lights and junctions which make them almost unusable at rush hour. At the end of the 1960s it was clear that a continuous ring road was necessary so the Boulevard *Périphérique* was constructed. This is known as 'le *Périphérique*' or even 'le Périph'. It is a 30 km circle around Paris that demarcates the geographical limit of the city; everything beyond it lies in a new county. The area within the ring is known as 'Paris intra muros' or Paris within the city walls, even though the walls are no longer standing. The ring has a series of exits that allow you to head into a given part of Paris or out into the suburbs. These are known as 'portes'. Several 'portes' form the beginning of motorways out of the city. One of the first things to learn when navigating around Paris is the location and name of the principal 'portes'. For, if you don't know where the exit that you want lies, you may end up going the wrong way round the circle. The lanes of the *Périphérique* aren't referred to as northbound or westbound, but rather as inner and outer lanes – '*Périphérique* intérieur' and '*Périphérique* extérieur'. You are supposed to know that when you are on the inner lane, Paris is on your right as you go round and deduce your direction accordingly.

Seizième Paris is divided into 'arrondissements' or administrative districts. Prior to 1860, there were twelve 'arrondissements', but when Haussmann was asked to redesign the city he grabbed eleven outlying villages and made them part of Paris. In case you are at all interested, this increased the area of the city from 3,288 hectares to 7,088 hectares. Thus, since 1860 there have been twenty numbered 'arrondissements', which are arranged in a clockwise spiral that starts with the 1er, which is centred on the Louvre, and ends with the 20ème on the far right hand, or eastern side of the city. Each 'arrondissement' has its own character – for example, the 13ème is the Asian district, while the 8ème has all the expensive shops. The 'arrondissement' which seems to have the most famous reputation is the 16ème or *seizième*. For the 16ème is where the rich people live. While you can find some hugely expensive houses there, it is mostly made up of old-fashioned, well-constructed apartment buildings with magnificent front doors and marble hallways. These are inhabited by rich, chic people who wear their fur coats to walk their little dogs in the Bois de Boulogne. Concierges, and even maids, can still be spotted in the 16ème. Therefore, *seizième* is, or possibly used to be, an adjective that means rich and chic.

MISCELLANEOUS (BUT NECESSARY) TRAVEL WORDS

Adjectif How many UK cities have their own adjective to define their residents? Not that many. People can call themselves Londoners, or Liverpudlians, or Brummies, or Mancunians, but someone from Stoke-on-Trent or Moreton-in-Marsh would be hard put to come up with an adjective to describe themselves. In France, things couldn't be more different: wherever you come from, there is an *adjectif* ready and waiting to describe you. Dictionaries show lists of the principal ones, some of which you can guess, like 'Parisien' for Paris and 'Lyonnais' for Lyons. Others are far more obscure. The inhabitants of Bourges, a sizeable cathedral town in central France, are not called 'Bourgeois' as might be assumed.

They are known as 'Berruyers'. This is as hard to pronounce as it is to guess. Logic does not necessarily play a part in the selection process for these *adjectifs*. When we used to live in Neuilly, we were 'Neuilléens'. Inhabitants of Neuilly-Plaisance, which is somewhere else entirely, are called 'Nocéens'. There are *adjectifs* for the inhabitants of every single town, city and even village, however small. When the village has only a couple of hundred inhabitants they may not be used much, but they are there should they be needed.

These *adjectifs* are used far more often than their UK equivalents, especially to identify prominent sporting figures. In a newspaper article about the exploits of a sportsman in some event, the person will be referred to by his full name at the beginning of the piece. Later references tend often to use the adjective relating to the city of his birth. For example, Jean Alesi, who comes from Avignon, was invariably referred to as 'l'Avignonnais' in practically any article about him. As far as I know, no French female star hails from the town of Belcombe. This is probably a good thing as women from Belcombe are unfortunately known as 'Belcombaises'. This sounds remarkably like 'belle qu'on baise', which means 'beautiful woman who gets screwed'. I am sure that the French habit of describing people by their city of origin is inextricably linked with their obsession with place of birth – see LIEU DE NAISSANCE.

Ouistiti! Should you ever be asked by a French person to take their photo in front of some famous monument somewhere, it is useless to point their camera at them and invite them brightly to 'Say "cheese!"' For a start, if you stand in front of a mirror and say 'cheese' with a silly French accent, it will not produce the photogenic rictus that you were hoping for. The main problem, however, is that a French tourist will not be expecting to be asked to say 'cheese' because in France, when being photographed, people say '*Ouistiti!*' The success of the photograph depends on the accent used: if you say '*Ouistiti*' – it means marmoset by the way – in a flat English accent reminiscent of the cartoon dog Droopy, you will look thoroughly miserable in the photo. If, on the other hand, you say it enthusiastically in a strong French accent, the last two syllables force your mouth sideways into a broad grin. Just in case you are planning on asking a French person to take your photo one day, there is a chance that instead of '*Ouistiti*' he may let his fondness for things culinary win through and ask you to say 'Omelette!'

Perpète les Oies France seems to lack the really extraordinary place names that you find in the UK. This perhaps explains why the French have devised some striking terms for places whose name they can't remember and for places they can't be bothered to call by their proper names. If someone wants to convey how far away and off the beaten track a place is, they will call it *Perpète les Oies*. If someone has bought a cottage hidden away in a small village miles from Paris, this will be described as 'Il a acheté une petite maison à *Perpète les Oies.*' *Perpète* means miles away while *les Oies* – the geese – shows how rural it is. If, on the other hand, you want to convey not so much how far away it is, but just the fact that the place in question is somewhere or other, it doesn't really matter where, you would call the place 'Trifouillis les Oies'. Telling someone that you had to go somewhere or other, a fair way away, in order to find what you were looking for, would be 'J'ai dû aller à Trifouillis les Oies pour le trouver.' 'Trifouillis' probably comes from the verb 'trifouiller' which means to rummage about.

Verge I have put this word in at the end, not because I believe that you necessarily need to know it before going to France – though this may depend on what sort of thing you do on your holidays – but rather so that you can appreciate why French people find a common UK road sign particularly amusing. For *verge* is the word for the male sexual organ. No wonder French holidays makers driving along the British countryside are much amused by signs warning you to beware 'Soft verges'.

Education

Here are some useful words about education because on holiday you may find yourself talking to locals who, given the fondness of the French for boasting about their offspring's prowess, may well try to regale you with tales of their educational success.

After school, the road to higher education in France is longer and harder than it is in the UK, and higher and further education are surprisingly different from the UK equivalents: the exams are different, the marking system is different and the reports are different. Even the reference books are different, as we will see.

You will discover a handy French term for going back to school and marvel at the fact that you can call yourself an intellectual and no one will laugh.

SCHOOL

Bac 'Le *Bac*', the familiar form of 'le Baccalauréat', is a word that strikes terror into the hearts of both schoolchildren and their parents. 'Le *Bac*' is the exam that you take at the end of your secondary education and roughly corresponds to A Levels. In my day, in England, when you reached the sixth form at the tender age of fifteen or so, you were expected to select the three subjects that you were going to concentrate on for the next two years. In my case, the subjects I chose, and fairly rapidly regretted, were maths, physics and chemistry. For two long years I studied nothing but these three subjects – apart from doing Use of English to make sure I could at least read and write, plus a bit of sport now and again. In France things are quite different. You can select between three main types of *Bac* – *Bac* S, *Bac* ES and *Bac* L – but, whichever you choose, you will study a wide range of at least eight subjects. In addition to your principal subjects – maths if you go for a *Bac* S (considered by many to be the elite among *Bacs*), economics and maths if you opt for a *Bac* ES, and literature should you decide on a *Bac* L – you will also study and be marked on other subjects including history, geography, two modern languages, sport (yes, there is a sport exam that counts for the final total) and even philosophy. There are written exams for all except sport, as well as orals for the modern languages. Marks out of 20 are attributed for each subject according to the most arcane of systems – see COEFFICIENT – and the total mark is also given out of 20. You need 10 or more to pass. The important thing is that you have to do sufficiently well in your favourite subjects in order to ensure that your weaker subjects don't bring down your average too much. Passing the exam – 'avoir son *Bac*' – is enough for most people. However, getting marks that are well above average will lead to various levels of distinction, namely 'assez bien', 'bien' and 'très bien', known collectively as '*Bac* avec mention'. Any one of these looks good on a CV and may help in later life.

Coefficient This is a tough one! In important exams in France, notably 'le BAC' but also in university exams, you have the extraordinary situation where marks for different papers do not all count the same. Each paper is given a sort of weighting that is usually expressed as a number between 1 and 8. When the paper has been marked and the candidate has scored, for example, 12 out of a possible 20, the mark is multiplied by the *coefficient* – often shortened to 'coef' – to give a final mark for that paper. Some subjects are heavily weighted – for example maths – while others have a 'coef' of 1 or 2 – for example sport. This means that if your offspring is very good at lower-weighted subjects and not so good at maths, he or she will be in trouble. Conversely, the happy few whose favourite subjects have the highest 'coef' can generally relax and put their feet up when it comes to taking the other subjects. From the very first parent–teacher meeting at the start of the 'Baccalauréat', everyone is made aware of the various *coefficients* and thus spends the next two years worrying. The weightings of the subjects vary enormously between the three main types of 'Baccalauréat'. This should definitely encourage you to select the one that best suits your children's talents in order to increase his or her chances of success.

La rentrée This single word is one of the most typical of the French language. In its literal sense *la rentrée* corresponds to the notion of 'going back to school'. French people can't understand how we can manage without a proper single word to describe this event as they have. In shops you see signs urging you to buy school supplies and children's clothes 'pour *la rentrée*'. In most houses, *la rentrée* strikes terror into everyone's hearts. The children hate it because it means the end of the long summer holidays. The parents don't like it much because it means several trips to the shops to buy books, files, pens and all the other essentials which seem to have vanished since the end of the previous summer term.

However, the concept of *la rentrée* is much broader than that. As well as the return to school or university, *la rentrée* covers the whole post-holiday period which spans the end of August to the first half of September. There are people for whom it extends well into October. In fact, you can use *la rentrée* to cover pretty much any time after your own return from holiday. For example, if you are faced at work with something that you don't want to deal with in June, you can say, 'On verra ça à *la rentrée*' – we will deal with that after the holidays. The lack of precision in this example is an advantage to the person who is putting whatever it is off until as late a date as possible. At home, the term is used as well for fixing engagements. Your friends will probably go away for a large part of the summer, though not necessarily at the same time as you, and therefore it is possible that you won't see them from the end of June to the beginning of September. The last thing you will say to each other will be along the lines of 'Vous viendrez dîner à *la rentrée*' – we'll see you for supper after the holidays. This shows that you want to see them but aren't that keen to fix a date at this stage.

Philosophie Whichever type of BAC exam you choose to sit, it will include a philosophy paper. This is known as 'l'épreuve de *philosophie*', or more commonly as 'l'épreuve de philo'. When I first heard of this I had the greatest difficulty in accepting the fact that children studying all disciplines should be expected to sit a philosophy exam. Not only does everyone have to do it, whether they are specializing in maths, literature or economics, but the subject itself is one of national importance. For, in June, when the BAC takes place, one of the major topics on the evening news on the day of the philosophy paper (and everyone sits the exam on the same day) is the questions set that year. To show what school-children are faced with, here are three questions from recent philo papers:

- L'ennui est-il caractéristique de l'être humain, ou de certaines époques de l'histoire?
- L'idée de pauvreté se réduit-elle à une catégorie économique?
- Peut-on s'attendre à tout?

Sécher You probably know the principal sense of the verb *sécher*, which is to dry, like for example, things that are left out in the sun. However, in the context of education, *sécher* takes on other meanings. For a start, if you feel when you get up in the morning that you really can't face going to school and decide to skive off (or bunk off, or whatever it was you said at your school), you would be said to '*sécher* les cours'. But the word also means to dry up metaphorically when you have no idea of how to reply to a teacher's question. Pupils are heard to exclaim despairingly, 'Je sèche' when faced with a question they can't answer, or to mutter darkly when asked how their day went, 'J'ai séché en maths.' If they don't want to get stuck and find themselves thinking 'je sèche' during a test, they may decide to cheat and prepare what we used to call a crib sheet, a hidden piece of paper with helpful notes written on it. In French this is known as an 'anti-sèche'. This term can still be used in later life – colleagues who are getting ready for a tough meeting are sometimes heard to say, 'Je prépare mon anti-sèche.'

Soleil Those of you who were bored in tedious science lessons at school will know the pastime of typing long numbers into a calculator which, when the calculator is turned upside down, reveal a word. For those who never did that sort of thing, a calculator 4 looks like an 'H' when upside down, 3, 5, 7 and 8 making respectively E, S, L and B. The longest word we came up with was shelloil, which isn't all that funny. You won't be surprised to learn that French students while away boring lectures in just the same way. They come up with words like *soleil* – sun – but also with 'elle bese'. 'Elle bese' is a lot funnier than shelloil because it sounds like 'elle baise'. 'Elle baise', as we will see under BAISER in Section 9, means she bonks.

Table des matières In an English book, the Contents page is right at the front. This is handy because you can open the book, look at the Contents and then carry on leafing through in the same direction until you reach the chapter that you are looking for. The French motto when it comes to books appears to be 'Why be logical?' because they put their *Table des matières* at the end of the book. This means you have to open it at the back, spot the chapter you want and then scramble in the opposite direction searching for it. The only possible explanation for putting the *Table des matières* at the back is so that, when you finish the book, you can scan through the list and think, 'Oh yes! I enjoyed Chapters 7 and 12.'

Tiret There are two quick ways of telling whether a book is English or French. (We shall suppose, for the sake of argument, that you have become so perfectly bilingual that you no longer notice whether words are French or English.) First, when books are standing upright in a bookcase: if you have to tilt your head to the right to read the wording down the spine, the book is English; if you tilt your head to the left, it is French. Please spare me a thought, sitting here checking my bookcase to test the theory for you and getting a sore neck. Why French printers print their spines the wrong way round is unclear. It is certainly illogical because it makes checking across a bookshelf, from left to right, in search of a particular book very uncomfortable. The second way to spot the origin of a book is to look at how conversation is displayed. In an English book you will see, for example:

'Isn't this a brilliant description of things French?' Sarah exclaimed admiringly.

Whereas in French, there will be a dash instead of an inverted comma, and a spoken sentence will look like this:

– En effet, s'écria Sébastien, C'est vraiment génial!

Conversations in novels begin with a dash, known as 'un *tiret*', a word I learned when one of my wife's aunts confessed that she only read the bits of a novel that started with a dash, 'Je ne lis que là où il y a des *tirets*.'

20 One of the first things you have to learn about education – whether primary, secondary or higher – in France, is that all marks for tests or exams are given out of a possible score of 20. At school, each child has an ongoing average mark, based on tests, homework and continuous assessment, which is always out of 20. Notions that were common at school in England in my day, such as coming top in Maths, being equal third in geography, or coming bottom in history, are almost unknown in France. People tend to remember the marks their children get in the principal subjects and then, assuming they are something you can be proud of (and not, as equally often happens, to be completely ashamed of), they regale their friends and acquaintances with tales of little François's brilliance in, for example, maths. It is common to see a group of women (men don't seem to do this) travelling on public transport and being driven to distraction by one of them boasting about the excellent marks of her marvellous offspring. For example, 'François a eu 18 en maths cette année!' – François got 18 in maths this year. Clearly, this bragging is all the more rewarding if she knows or suspects that her audience's children have not achieved the same dizzy heights of academic success. Indeed, the bigger the gulf between the respective children's marks, the more fun the game.

AFTER THE BAC

Classe préparatoire In the UK, you take your A Levels, or whatever they are called now, and, if you get the right grades, you go straight off to university, whatever course you have chosen. In France, you can do this too. However, if you want to become an engineer, which means going to one of the GRANDES ÉCOLES, or if you are aiming for one of the elite schools of literature or business, you have to attend a *classe préparatoire*. This involves spending two years (or three if you fail the exams) in a special Lycée immediately after passing your 'Baccalauréat'. Of course, no one calls it *classe préparatoire*, just 'prépa'. Proud parents, in reply to your enquiry as to what their offspring are doing at the moment, will say things like 'Il est en prépa au Lycée Louis-Le-Grand' – Louis-Le-Grand in Paris being one of the better Lycées. Your chances of getting into the best GRANDES ÉCOLES are, of course, considerably improved if you go to one of the top Lycées to do your 'prépa'. Indeed, in later life, people are more likely to name-drop about their 'prépa' than about their ordinary Lycée. *Classe préparatoire* being terribly elitist, they have all sorts of in terms for the courses, or for redoing one of the years. For example, if you are preparing to do engineering, the first and second years may be known as 'Hypotaupe' and 'Taupe' respectively, while should you be hoping to study literature later on, your classes will be referred to as 'Hypokhâgne' (pronounced 'ipokyne') and 'Khâgne'.

Gadzart If you don't holiday in France all that often, you will very likely never hear these words. I include them only because they illustrate the cult side of French higher education. As we will see with x, the French like to give insider names to people who have attended their top universities. The engineering school with one of the best reputations is the École Nationale Supérieure d'Arts et Métiers, often known simply as 'Les Arts'. *Gadzart* – a shortened form of 'un GARS des Arts' (GARS means bloke) – is the name for one of its pupils. If you are lucky enough to be one, you can count on the support of other past pupils once you leave and will thus receive preferential treatment when applying for a job and when moving upward in your career. You hear colleagues explaining someone's meteoric rise in a company by saying, 'C'est normal: c'est un *Gadzart*.'

Another well-known term for pupils of a top university is 'Énarque.' This is someone who has attended the elite École Nationale d'Administration and who will probably end up a Member of Parliament, or even Prime Minister. The ENA's ambitions are modestly summed up in its motto: 'La formation des décideurs publics de demain' – training tomorrow's policy-makers.

Grandes Écoles
In the UK, if you want higher education, there is nowhere better than one of the top universities. French universities are OK in their way, but if you want a qualification that is going to set you up in later life, you are going to have to attend one of the *Grandes Écoles*. 'École' in this context doesn't mean school as in high school but rather a place of education. *Grandes Écoles* specialize in either science – in which case they are known as 'Écoles d'ingénieurs' – business studies or commerce. Famous *Grandes Écoles* include ENA – École Nationale d'Administration – HEC – Hautes Études Commerciales – and École Polytechnique (see x). If all goes well, you spend three years at a *Grande École*. But, in order to get in, you have to spend two years in a CLASSE PRÉPARATOIRE, which means that a French engineering degree, for example, requires five years' study rather than the three it takes in the UK.

Maths sup, maths spé
If you are aiming to get into one of the elite engineering schools, the two years you have to spend at the CLASSE PRÉPARATOIRE will involve studying a huge amount of maths. The first and second years of the course are respectively

known as 'mathématiques supérieures' and 'mathématiques spécialisées' and are notoriously tough. Indeed, students work so hard
that many barely see the light of day for two years. As usual, no
one ever refers to these two years as 'mathématiques supérieures'
and 'mathématiques spécialisées'. Proud parents, and the students
themselves, invariably shorten the terms to *maths sup*, *maths spé*.
Unfortunately, the first time (or even the second) someone informs
you that they are doing 'matsoup matspay', there is no way on
earth that you will understand that they are spending two horrendous years 'twixt school and university studying higher mathe-
matics.

X Imagine that you are going to see someone for the first time at
a business meeting and you ask your colleague what the person is
like. If they reply that 'Il a fait l'X' or that he is 'X Mines', will you
be any the wiser? Even if you have heard of the most elite of all
French engineering schools, the *ne plus ultra* of GRANDES ÉCOLES
that is the École Polytechnique, will you make the connection?
École Polytechnique, a redoubtable mix of Sandhurst and Cam-
bridge where pupils are as much soldiers as students, has absolutely
nothing in common with a British polytechnic. The entrance exam,
which is taken after two years of CLASSE PRÉPARATOIRE, preferably at the best Lycée, assuming you can get in, is the toughest of
all. If you survive the course, however, the deference of your peers is
assured and you are made for life. École Polytéchnique is generally
known by the abbreviation X. This comes from the emblem of the
school, which shows two cannons crossed in the shape of an X. The
'Mines' part refers to the specialization during the course, as
opposed, for example, to 'Ponts' or bridges. 'Mines' or mining is
without doubt the acme of French education. Being the beneficiaries

of the best French education, 'X Mines' have a very high opinion of themselves and a correspondingly low opinion of everyone else. I know several 'X Mines', only two of whom I can count as friends.

AND LATER

Ingénieur I discovered that I was an *ingénieur* well before I was entirely sure what one was. While the word means engineer, it has a whole spirit and history that the English one doesn't have. Where the word engineer is used fairly generously in English to cover both people who know something about engineering and people who have nothing whatsoever to do with it, its use in French is much more strictly regulated. You don't find dustmen in France being called refuse engineers and the bloke who comes to service our boiler would never claim to be a heating engineer. To be called 'un *ingénieur*' in France you have to have an engineering degree to back it up. Engineering degrees come only from 'une école d'*ingénieurs*' and preferably from one of the GRANDES ÉCOLES.

Intellectuel One of the amazing differences between France and the UK is that a French person can define themselves seriously as an intellectual and not require any further job description, even less be thought pretentious. When there are discussion programmes on the TV, or even demonstrations in the street, some of the participants will be exclusively described as being 'des *intellectuels*'. In the UK, they would be called writers, or professors or whatever. If you look the word up in a French dictionary, the definition is someone whose life is devoted to 'les activités de l'esprit', i.e. someone who spends their time thinking. Apparently, one famous French thinker, whose name escapes me, put down *intellectuel* as his occupation on his passport and no one found this in the least odd. Why not give it a go when you next apply for one?

Service National This is not really pertinent as National Service no longer exists in France, but, when I first came here, it was a hot topic of discussion among friends and relatives of my age. As no one was particularly keen to spend a year pretending to be a soldier and putting off the day when they could start earning some money, the words I heard were mainly related to how to get out of doing it. One of the words people wanted to hear was 'réformé', which meant you were excused *Service National* because you were considered unsuitable in some way: flat feet, asthma or whatever. Better still was 'exempté', which also meant you were excused but without specifying any shortcomings, whether physical or psychological. This was the ideal escape because there was no adverse judgement on you nor any stain on your character. The one to avoid was, seemingly, P4, the lowest psychological evaluation, which meant that you were let off because you were frankly too bonkers. Nevertheless, many young people went to great lengths to pretend that they were potty – favourite ruses included standing on their head for hours or pretending they couldn't actually speak – so that they would be let off as P4. Unfortunately, they forgot that the evaluation would follow them for the rest of their careers.

If you couldn't get out of *Service National*, you probably spent the year looking forward to 'la quille', the end of your time as a soldier, when you were finally set free.

Entertainment and Sport

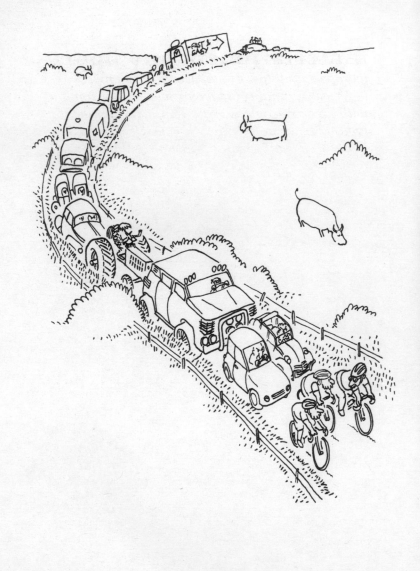

In this section, you will discover a selection of words relating to various spectator activities.

As well as finding out why going to a pantomime with French people is a risky business and what a typical French dog is called, you will learn how best to encourage a French sports team and what to do if they win.

FILMS AND CINEMAS

Atmosphère Certain quotes from films seem to be heard remarkably frequently in France. Where I first worked, whenever anyone used the word *atmosphère* – which means, unsurprisingly, roughly what it means in English – one or other of my colleagues would mutter in a shrill, fake Parisian accent, '*Atmosphère, atmosphère . . .*' None of my other colleagues showed any surprise at this, nor did anyone think to offer me any explanation as to why they did it. After I had heard it several times, I made an effort to discover what it was all about. It turns out to be part of a famous quote from a 1938 French film called *Hôtel du Nord*. This is a place that still exists, standing on the banks of the Canal St Martin in Paris. The words are spoken by an actress known simply as Arletty: '*Atmosphère, atmosphère*! Est-ce que j'ai une gueule d'*atmosphère*?' in a shrill, authentic Parisian accent.

Bizarre This is another word that comes from a famous film quote. In the same way that mentioning ATMOSPHÈRE prompts people to imitate Arletty, using the word *bizarre* generally causes someone nearby to say something like '*Bizarre*? Vous avez dit *bizarre*? Comme c'est *bizarre*.' The line comes from a well-known film called *Drôle de drame* starring Louis Jouvet and Michel Simon. Jouvet says to Simon, 'Moi j'ai dit *bizarre*? Comme c'est *bizarre*!' You may find that you use the word *bizarre* quite often, so beware! If you get ATMOSPHÈRE and *bizarre* in the same sentence when talking to a group of film buffs, you will never hear the end of it.

Médor If there is a dog in a classic 1950s British film, there is a fair chance that it will be called Rover. Similarly, in children's programmes that involve farmyard animals, the horse will probably be named Dobbin – and this despite the fact that no living horse is called that, nor probably ever has been – while the cow will be Buttercup. Should there be a cat in a story, it may well be called Tiddles, a hamster, if present, being known as Hammy. The French equivalent of Rover is *Médor*, though I know of no one who has ever met a dog of that name. However, at the time when we drove a Rover car, we thought it hilarious to refer to it as *Médor*. Extensive research has revealed that a French horse in an old film might well be called 'Pom Pom', thought people seem much more certain that the cow would be called 'Marguerite'. Tiddles, the cat, would probably be known as 'Minou'. Sadly, there seems to be less affection for hamsters in France because there is apparently no common name for them.

Ouvreuse You would think that going to the cinema in France would be essentially the same as doing so in the UK. Unfortunately, things are rarely as simple as they seem. The first time I set foot in a French cinema – a particularly flash one on the Champs Élysées – we were shown to our seats by an *ouvreuse* or usherette. She had taken the tickets from us at the door and then handed them back by our seats, leaving her hand outstretched. While I was still wondering what the girl was up to, my wife produced a coin of some sort and gave it to her. She accepted it with minimum gratitude and left us. Thus, I discovered that you are expected to tip a cinema usherette. Tipping in cinemas is now much less common than it used to be, but you will definitely be expected to tip in most theatres and even in sports stadiums. A good way of passing the time, while you are waiting for the show to begin, is to watch each patron as they arrive and see if you can guess by the girl's reaction how much or how little she has been tipped. You will also be able to get a rough idea of how much she earns in an hour and thus understand why jobs as *ouvreuses* in fashionable theatres are much in demand.

OTHER FORMS OF ENTERTAINMENT

Pantomime In French this word describes a show based on mime. What we in the UK call a pantomime is unknown in France. This came to light when we went with some French friends to a traditional English pantomime in Paris. Sitting waiting for the show to begin, we carefully went through the helpful programme notes with our friends Christophe and Hélène to explain what you are expected to shout out and when. We made it clear that the choice was limited to 'He's behind you' and 'Oh, no he isn't', and that this was done only at specific times. They almost, almost grasped it. At a key moment, when the wicked Vizir was about to have Aladdin executed, people in the audience, visibly moved, were calling out things like 'No! No!' It was at this point that Christophe decided to take his first steps in audience participation, choosing the quietest of moments to call out the immortal words 'Mind ze dog!' The result was astonishing: the actors stopped dead. Silence and confusion reigned both on stage and among the audience, for there was no dog anywhere to be seen. Christophe, oblivious to all this, beamed proudly, the play resumed, and Aladdin, you will be relieved to hear, was not executed.

Télévision I include this word, not because I believe that you don't know what it means, but rather as a pretext for saying publicly how absolutely appalling French television is. Indeed, I don't really know which is harder: explaining to the French how awful their television programmes are, or persuading Brits that they should be far more grateful to those concerned for providing the best channels in the world. I could give you chapter and verse to justify my assertion that French TV (with the possible exception of the ARTE channel) is rubbish, but it wouldn't change anything. So I won't bother. It is not worth it.

SPORTING MATTERS

Chants des supporteurs We will see later (see VIRAGES) where the true French football supporters congregate. What they do while the match is going on is no different from what their British counterparts do: they chant. More particularly, they chant some fairly unflattering things. For example, when a goalkeeper is getting ready to take a goal kick, there is a collective cry of 'Oh! Hisse . . .' as he makes his run-up, followed by a long-drawn-out cry of 'Enculés!' as the ball flies down the field. 'Enculés' – typing this is a new experience – means something like you buggers and is directed at the opposing fans. When the home team is winning, or has won, their supporters taunt the losing fans by singing, 'Et ils sont où, et ils sont où, et ils sont où les . . . ?' – where have they gone? – filling in the name of the opposing team at the end. When things are going well for one team, their fans will be on their feet cheering and chanting, 'Qui n'est pas debout n'est pas . . .' – whoever isn't standing up doesn't support . . . – whichever team we are talking about. Lyons supporters have their own variation: not only do they stand, but they bounce up and down chanting, 'Qui ne saute pas n'est pas Lyonnais' – whoever isn't bouncing isn't a Lyons supporter. Of course, the poor referee can come in for special attention, especially when he makes controversial decisions. Those unhappy with his efforts shout, 'Aux CHIOTTES l'arbitre!' – stick the ref in the bogs!

Cheval The correct translation of to ride a horse is 'monter à *cheval*'. There are, however, people who say 'faire du *cheval*'. It is probably not a good idea to lend your horse to that sort of person.

Cocorico French cockerels do not go cock-a-doodle-doo in the manner of their British cousins; they go *cocorico*. More interestingly, French people use *cocorico*, or possibly 'coquerico', as a victory cry. This may well be because the cockerel is the symbol of French sporting teams (see FANFARE). Announcing a victory, a person or a newpaper headline will start with *cocorico* before going on to specify what the victory was. '*Cocorico!* On a gagné une médaille d'or!' The word can also be used as a synonym for victory; for example, you could describe an uninspiring victory as 'un petit *cocorico*'.

Cyclistes This is not so much a word as a concept that you have to learn early on, especially if you plan on driving anywhere in France on a Sunday morning. Cyclists in France are firmly convinced that roads exist for their sole benefit, to the exclusion of all other road users. This conviction is particularly evident on Sunday mornings. Not only do French cyclists resolutely cycle two or three abreast so that they can chat to each other, thus forcing any following car to drive at 25kmh, but also, and more disturbingly, they believe that their ownership of the road is dependent on their wearing extremely brightly coloured and, quite honestly, far from flattering, Lycra suits. Pick a stretch of road near any patch of greenery on a Sunday morning and you will be amazed by the number of dazzlingly dressed cyclists you will spot and hear shouting to each other – particularly if it's early in the morning. I have a theory that, when I am out cycling in jeans and a T-shirt, the likelihood of another cyclist greeting me is inversely proportional to the garishness of his Lycra and the sophistication of his wraparound sunglasses.

Fanfare If you are going to a Six Nations rugby match at the Stade de France, try to catch the RER the *fanfare* is travelling on. This is a group of brass-instrument-wielding fans who sit together in the stadium and urge on their team with bursts of strident, cheery music. Each crowd of supporters usually includes at least two *fanfares*, and they use the trip to the stadium as a warm-up practice. Even a small brass band can really make its presence felt in a confined carriage, especially when they and the accompanying fans start bouncing up and down with the beat.

If you can't find the carriage with the brass band, try to get on the one with the cockerel – though this is admittedly not easy unless you're travelling at daybreak. The emblem of the French team is a cockerel – 'le coq' – and one or two fanatical supporters like to turn up at the stadium with a live cockerel, which they let loose on the pitch at the start of the game. The poor thing spends much of the match wandering aimlessly about, dodging balls and charging players, until it is recaptured and taken home to recover. It is not clear whether the cockerel accompanies the fans to the bar after the match – see TROISIÈME MI-TEMPS.

Les bleus Whatever the sport, be it football, rugby or basketball, the French national team always wear blue shirts. They are therefore, unimaginatively, known as *les bleus*. *L'Équipe* newspaper and match reports on news bulletins refer to *les bleus'* performance and the supporters' cry, 'Allez *les bleus*!', works whatever the sport involved. It can either be shouted out as encouragement or, at moments of particular fervour, expanded into a repetitive song:

> Allez *les bleus*!
> Allez *les bleus*!
> Allez!
> Allez *les bleus*!
> Allez *les bleus*!
> Allez!

This is easy to pick up and streets ahead of the dreadful English football chant that goes 'En-ger-land; En-ger-land!'

People leaving work on the evening of an important match will stick their heads round colleagues' doors to say, 'Allez les *bleus* pour ce soir!' and expect enthusiastic agreement.

Nous Convincing proof, should such really be needed, that the French are more chauvinistic than the British is provided by the fact that, whereas the British commentator of a televised sporting event always refers to the home team as they or the British, the French TV commentator says *nous*.

Sports The only name of a sport that seems to be exactly the same in French and English is rugby. However, as the word is generally used only by players or commentators who come from the far south-west corner of France, it is pronounced 'rrruugby'. While football is also 'football' in French, hardly anyone, of course, calls it that. It is known simply as 'le foot', and a game is 'un match de foot'. Basketball and handball (a sport that is widely popular in France but little known in the UK) have identical proper names in French but again are shortened to 'basket' and 'hand' so that people go to 'un match de basket', not 'un match de basketball'. The ball is not 'un football' but 'un ballon de foot'. Volleyball, another game that is far more popular in France than in the UK, is known as 'le volley', and the ball is 'un ballon de volley'. Cricket is strictly 'le cricket' in French but the only people who say the word are in fact getting it mixed up with croquet and so it doesn't count. This is perhaps a good moment to give you some excellent advice: never even think about attempting to explain the rules of cricket to a French person.

Tiercé You have to learn a lot of horseracing-related terms to sit through the news on France Info, for the evening bulletins often mention the day's *tiercé* result. Whereas in England you tend to back a single horse to win or place, and refer to it by name, in France, you not only back horses by referring to their number on the racecard, you also tend to bet in groups. A *tiercé* is a bet on the first three horses in a given race. You study the racecard, make your choice and predict first, second and third by their numbers. After the race the results will be read out: 'Les résultats du *tiercé* à Saint Cloud: le 15, le 7 et le 11' and that's it. No names of the horses at all, and you only win your bet if you have got the three correct numbers in order. If you have the correct numbers in the wrong order, you win less. There are also special races which require predicting the first four or even five horses. These are called 'quarté' and 'quinté'. Incidentally, most of the *tiercé* races are not run at a gallop on the flat or over jumps, but at a trot pulling a lightweight cart (called 'un sulky'), like in the USA. If you want to bet on a *tiercé*, you can do it in a special bar for horseracing fanatics which is called a PMU (Pari Mutuel Urbain), though such bars are generally smokier and dirtier than ordinary ones.

Troisième mi-temps It takes only one expression to show that French rugby supporters are made of different stuff from football fans. *La troisième mi-temps* – the third half-time – refers to the time spent in the pub after the match has ended. What is important about this is that supporters from both teams get together and enjoy a beer or six, without anybody even remotely contemplating beating each other up. This is particularly evident after a Six Nations rugby match, when the bars near the Stade de France fill up with fans of both nationalities whose only common language is beer and who, because of this, get along famously. I have often witnessed a lone fan ordering a round of beer in a bar after a good rugby game, sure in the knowledge that others will shortly come and join him.

Vélo Another disappointment! I remember learning at school that the French word for bicycle was 'bicyclette'. I needn't have bothered: no one uses the word. The two-wheeled device, beloved of Lycra-clad Sunday-morning sportsmen, is known as 'un *vélo*'. This is an abbreviation of the old word 'vélocipède'. A racing bike is 'un *vélo* de course' and a mountain bike is 'un VTT', which stands for 'un *vélo* tous terrains'. This is perhaps a good moment to point out that many English books about France and the French will have you believe that a common French term for a bicycle is 'la petite reine' or the little queen. This may have been the case fifty years ago, but it certainly isn't now. Not only have I never heard the expression used by anybody, but a brief survey showed that several people I asked didn't even know what the term meant.

Virages At football grounds, notably at the Parc des Princes where Paris Saint-Germain plays, the really ardent supporters congregate in the corners of the stadium, where it bends. Logically, these areas are known as 'les *virages*' – the bends. Depending on how fervently you support your team, not to mention how much you fancy a good punch-up after the match, you will either actively seek out, or take great care to avoid, 'les *virages*'.

Paperwork

If there is one thing that should make you think twice about moving to France, it is the paperwork. For there really is an awful lot of it to be dealt with when you live here. If you are unconvinced on this point, you merely have to check the handy guides to all the various 'cartes' and 'permis' that are on sale in newsagents and bookshops. Of course, if you just come on holiday, you won't need a resident's permit or an identity card or find yourself having to tell someone your place of birth. Furthermore, you will never need to have a stressful encounter with a French civil servant at their unhelpful best. And what a loss that is!

There is a section on French weddings which may come in handy if you are ever invited to one. Having read it, you will realize that you have all the French vocabulary you need to get married here yourself, should you wish to. You will also find out why you shouldn't expect to receive a slice of French wedding cake by post.

The section ends with tips on how to sell a car and the real reason why you should give blood in France.

DOCUMENTS

Carte d'identité In France, everyone has to have, and carry, some form of identification. This identification is not necessarily a passport. All French people, whether they travel abroad or not, have to have an identity card or *carte d'identité*. Not long ago, as well as the holder's personal details including his date of birth and the all-important place of birth and a photo, the identity card even included the holder's index-finger print, something I found absolutely astonishing when I spotted it on my wife's card. Nowadays identity cards are plastic-covered and supposed to be tamper-proof. The fact that all French people have to carry at least an identity card explains why cheque cards don't exist in France. In the UK, where you don't necessarily have any official form of identity document, cheque cards were devised as proof that the person signing the cheque was indeed who they claimed to be. The person receiving the cheque compared the signatures on the back of the card and on the cheque to be sure that all was well. In France, when you pay by cheque, you invariably hear the cashier ask for 'une pièce d'identité, s'il vous plaît' – some kind of formal identification. This can be your identity card, your passport or your driving licence – or, for very large sums, all three – and the cashier writes down the reference number of the proffered document on the back of the cheque.

Carte de séjour At present even citizens of one of the states of the European Union require a *carte de séjour* or resident's permit. In order to get one, you must have been in a job for at least three months as three months' payslips are required as proof of regular employment. You also need your passport, some photos and a phone or electricity bill as a 'justification de domicile' as evidence of where you live. You take all these to your local sous-préfecture (regional town hall), where you will spend the morning queuing and filling in forms. If any of your photocopied documents is not considered up to scratch, you will be sent away to get another one. This means queuing all over again another day. Once the form-filling has been completed correctly, you will have to wait several weeks for a 'convocation', which is a summons to return to the sous-préfecture to do some more queuing, before finally being given your *carte de séjour*. This is a plastic card which lists your personal details and includes the unflattering photo that you provided and which now looks even worse than before. Many years ago, my first *carte de séjour* had the words 'Police de Paris' conspicuously printed across the top. I used to take great delight in brandishing it in response to a request for proof of identity, trying to imitate the way policemen on TV flash their warrant cards at suspects. It hardly ever impressed anybody.

Fonctionnaire French civil servants, or government employees in general, are known as *fonctionnaires* and enjoy a reputation similar to that of their colleagues in the UK. They lead a peaceful life and, if that's at all threatened by proposed government legislation, come out on strike with impunity. True civil servants are referred to as 'ronds de cuir', which is a reference to the round leather cushion found on old-fashioned office chairs. As a foreigner, you are most likely to encounter *fonctionnaires* when you want to obtain a CARTE DE SÉJOUR. I recommend that you adopt the strategy devised by my wife for getting on the good side of a *fonctionnaire* from the moment of your first encounter. This consists in saying, right at the beginning, in as sincere a voice as you can muster, 'Mon Dieu! Vous avez énormément de travail!' – Goodness! You are *extremely* busy – whether they appear to be doing anything or not. It works wonders! The collective term for a plurality of French *fonctionnaires* is 'l'administration'. This all-purpose term covers the Civil Service and bureaucracy in general and is heard only when someone is complaining about something.

Impossible There is an expression used to demonstrate how resolute and wonderful the French believe themselves to be: '*Impossible* n'est pas français!' – impossible isn't the French way. Whenever a person is faced with a tricky problem and someone suggests that it is impossible, whoever it is may well use the expression to show that no way is he going to give up and be beaten. However, it seems that only French people are allowed to use it of themselves. I discovered this when faced with a recalcitrant civil servant – see FONCTIONNAIRE – who was telling me that giving me a resident's permit on the strength of the papers I had presented was *impossible*. Thinking that the expression would provide a splendid and unarguable answer to the woman's objection, I said, 'Mais, je croyais qu'*impossible* n'était pas français' – but I thought that impossible wasn't the French way. Instead of being stunned by my erudition and agreeing that I was absolutely right and there was no need to fill in any more forms, the woman turned red in the face and shouted, 'Vous vous foutez de moi?' – Are you taking the piss? – and threatened to throw my file on the floor. Apologizing and getting her to calm down and reconsider my file took absolutely ages.

Lieu de naissance The difference between the numerous French forms that you have to fill in and English ones is easy to spot. And it has nothing at all to do with language. Pretty much any French formal document that you are required to complete – and heaven knows, there are a lot of them – includes in the list of your personal details not only your date of birth but also your place of birth, 'date et *lieu de naissance*'. In France, your birth certificate, passport, identity card, driving licence and LIVRET DE FAMILLE all specify your date and place of birth. Applying for a bank account, joining the local library, enrolling at a new school, applying for university, buying a house and a great number of other things, all require you to tell someone where you were born. As they are going to have to mention it so often, it is advisable, if you can possibly manage it, to make sure your children are born somewhere nice, preferably somewhere chic and expensive. This will improve their chances of success at practically anything in later life. We managed this brilliantly for our son, who was born in Neuilly – one of the smartest of Parisian suburbs – but did less well for our daughter, who was born in the 18ème 'arrondissement' of Paris despite the fact that we were living in the more upmarket 17ème at the time.

Nom de famille There seems to be disagreement in France as to which comes first – your first name or your surname. On the ever-present forms you keep filling, many specify 'Nom, prénom', asking you to fill in your '*nom de famille*' or surname first and your given name second. We could dispute the logic of this, but as it is their country and their forms, we won't, for the moment. At least when it occurs on a form, you can see which name is which, assuming the person has filled in the form correctly. What causes problems is when people introduce themselves. A considerable number of French people have been brought up to give their surname first and the first name second and will say something like 'Bonjour. Dupont, Jacques'. This is peculiar, perhaps, but not too tricky, because Dupont is a readily recognized surname and Jacques is easy to identify as a first name. Confusion arises when you are introduced to someone who has a surname that sounds like a first name – and there are loads of them. If someone shakes your hand and says 'Bonjour. Martin, Michel', you have no idea whether you are facing Monsieur Martin or Monsieur Michel. Worse, if you make an assumption based on your way of doing things, you may be with someone who assumes the opposite. I had a boss who believed in the surname-first technique, while I, resolutely, come from the surname-second school. When we were introduced to 'Georges, Martin', I spent the meeting thinking I was with M. Martin, but saying nothing, while my boss kept calling him M. Georges. In fact he really was M. Georges.

WEDDINGS

Livret de famille Marriage certificates as such don't exist in France. Proof that you really are married is provided by your *livret de famille*, a plastic-covered beige booklet, about the size of a big passport, issued by the mairie in the locality where you got married. After six pages of detailed notes on how to cope with the formalities relating to the various births and deaths that await you down the road of life, you come to the interesting bit, which is the 'extrait de l'Acte de Mariage'. On the left-hand page are set out the details of the 'époux' or bridegroom – his date of birth, place of birth and the names of his parents. Similar details of the 'épouse' or bride are on the opposite page. The date of the marriage is given, though it is usually partially obscured by a large and impressive stamp showing the name of the mairie where the wedding took place and by the Maire's often flamboyant signature. At the bottom of the page are the details of the 'contrat de mariage' or pre-nuptial agreement which the bride and groom may have chosen to enter into. This decides how your goods are to be divided up in the event of the death of one of the spouses or of a divorce. Whenever you buy property you will be asked for details of your 'contrat de mariage'. If you decided not to have a pre-nuptial agreement when you got married, you will have to reply to such questions by saying that you are ruled by the regulations known as 'séparation de biens', which I believe means a fair 50/50 share-out. The remaining pages of the *livret de famille* are for details of the date and place of birth of your children. There is room for up to eight offspring should you be energetic enough to require it!

Oui I include this not because it has some peculiar or exotic meaning other than the one that you learned at school but rather because it is the only word that you have to be able to pronounce in order to get married in France. This applies only if you have a civil wedding at 'la mairie'; a church wedding requires considerably more effort on the part of the bride and bridegroom. In a French civil marriage service everything hinges on this single word. Bride and groom have to say *oui* in reply to a long and convoluted question asked by Monsieur le Maire, and then the deed is done. In my case, as I wasn't going to have much to say, I wanted my *oui* to be as perfect as possible. So, the evening before the wedding, I was to be found or, rather, I was thankfully not found, in a distant corner of my future parents-in-law's huge garden saying *oui* out loud in a variety of tones until I hit upon one which sounded assured, positive yet friendly. I'm pleased to say that people commented on it in favourable terms after the ceremony.

Pièce montée One of the major differences between French and British weddings lies in the wedding cake. If you marry a French person, you can explain to your future family-in-law that what you want is a substantial fruit cake covered in white icing – preferably an assembly of three similar cakes of decreasing size – until you are blue in the face. You won't get one. What you will get is an extraordinary structure called 'une *pièce montée*'. This is usually a conical shape about 80cm high, made up of loads of small choux-pastry balls filled with vanilla cream and stuck together with sugared icing, topped off by charming little figures of a bride and bridegroom. When the time comes, rather than ceremoniously cutting the cake, the bride and groom break chunks off the *pièce montée* with their fingers and hand them out. Everybody gets about three pastry balls each. It is actually quite good and considerably lighter on the stomach than the British equivalent. The fact that the *pièce montée* has to be eaten on the day of the wedding because of the cream filling explains why friends and family from England who couldn't come to our wedding were disappointed not to receive a slice of cake by post.

FORMALITIES AND INSTITUTIONS

À jeun I encountered this when I gave blood for the first time in France. 'Soyez *à jeun*' it said on the friendly notice in the office calling for volunteers. 'Jeun' comes from 'jeûner', which means to fast. *À jeun* therefore means in a state of fasting, in other words, that you shouldn't have any breakfast. However, there are differing views about what strictly constitutes being *à jeun*. Those who tend to follow rules to the letter take it to mean that you shouldn't eat or drink anything whatsoever before doing whatever it is. French people, on the other hand, interpret the term more liberally and assume that, while they shouldn't eat a hearty breakfast, they can surely be allowed a cup of coffee or two to help them cope with the rigours of giving blood, or even just giving a blood sample. Certain medicines specify on the packet that they should be taken *à jeun*. This is generally construed to mean that you should swallow them with your first sip of coffee in the morning.

Chéquier 'Un *chéquier*' is a French chequebook. French cheque-books, as you will already have guessed, are not like UK ones. The first, most obvious difference is in their format. While UK cheque-books have the counterfoil to the left of the cheque, which gives a chequebook its long, bendy appearance, French ones have the counterfoil running along the top edge of the cheque. This gives the chequebook a more book-like feel, less long and less thin. It also makes it more rigid and helps it to fit into your pocket more neatly. The format of the cheques is also different: each cheque puts the amount first rather than the payee. French cheques have an extra line to fill in as they ask you to specify where the cheque was made out. If you look, you'll spot a little line down by the signature that reads simply 'à . . .' This is another example of the French obsession with the place where things happen. See LIEU DE NAISSANCE.

Donner du sang The large room in the converted tobacco factory where I used to give blood in Bristol was filled for the day with a number of rickety camp beds. After you had finished giving blood you were led to one of them and made to lie down. A charming nurse would then bring you a reviving cup of tea and a couple of custard cream biscuits. The plain surroundings and the simple tea seemed to increase the feeling of virtue that you derived from doing your social duty. Once you had finished your tea you went placidly back to work. Giving blood 'à la française' is not a matter of virtue; it is a gastronomic extravaganza. The donating procedure is similar to that used in the UK. The difference lies in what happens afterwards. There is no question of being led to a camp bed; even less is there talk of cups of tea. The nurse leads you to a table groaning under the weight of croissants, BAGUETTES, ham, 'saucisson', pickles and tomatoes and, most surprising of all, carafes of red wine. As I usually give blood in the early morning, I don't get much work done before mid-afternoon!

L'Argus When people start to talk about buying or selling a car in France you can be sure that *l'Argus* will be mentioned at some point. When I first heard friends or colleagues saying 'Je l'ai vendue à *l'Argus*,' I wondered who it was or, alternatively, where such a place might be. It turns out that *l'Argus* is neither a fanatical collector of second-hand cars nor a saleroom. It is a second-hand-car magazine that comes out every Thursday, lists models of car, set out by their year of manufacture, and gives their value for a variety of conditions. Therefore, 'vendre à *l'Argus*' means that you sold your car at the price specified for it in the magazine. Garages which are prepared to purchase your old car when you buy a new one will offer to buy it 'à *l'Argus*'. Depending on how keen they are to sell you the new one, they will sometimes go as far as offering 'Prix *Argus* + 10%', or less, if cars are selling well.

Lettre recommandée It is time for a wild generalization: the French are completely obsessed with registered letters. The full term for such things is 'une *lettre recommandée* avec accusé de réception' or registered letter with acknowledgement, and they are rarely used for good news. Sending or receiving a *lettre recommandée* is usually the sign that a conflict is looming or that you are in some sort of trouble. Even though a registered letter is resorted to so that there is proof that it has been delivered, there are always shady people, or 'petits malins' – cunning little guys – who push things to the limit. True 'petits malins' have been known to acknowledge receipt of a registered envelope but maintain that it didn't actually contain a letter at all. Faced with this sort of behaviour, someone devised a special registered envelope for hardened 'petits malins'. It is made of a sheet of card folded in two. You write the text of your letter on one side of the card, fold it and glue it closed. The whole thing is then stamped, addressed and registered. As the envelope *is* the letter, it is impossible for even the most duplicitous addressee to deny that he has received the contents. The sight of a registered letter can cause fear and trembling, even in those who have nerves of steel. The bell rang one Saturday morning and I opened the front door to see our postman, Marcel, at the front gate brandishing a large brown envelope. 'C'est une *lettre recommandée*,' he called cheerily. Before I could answer, or start walking towards him, Marcel continued in a calming, reassuring tone, 'Mais, c'est vos CHÉQUIERS. Ce n'est pas le Fisc' – it's your chequebooks; it's not the tax people. Having a clear conscience, it hadn't occurred to me that it might be the 'Fisc' and I asked him why he felt the need to mention it. Marcel animatedly explained that if he didn't tell people who the registered letter was from, they invariably panicked and assumed it was from the tax authorities. If people were out when he called, he left a card saying a registered letter was waiting to be picked up at the post office, but always added who it was from, otherwise people wouldn't come to collect it. According to Marcel, this sort of thing happens a lot in our village because of its number of wealthy inhabitants!

Livret A A staple of French life. Almost everyone has one. 'Un *Livret A*' is the basic French savings account. You can open one either at the equivalent of the Post Office Savings Bank – known simply as La Poste – or at the national savings bank, which is called La Caisse d'Épargne. Intended principally for small savers – the maximum you can save is €15,300 – a *Livret A* won't make you rich as the interest rate is currently just 2 per cent, but it is, thankfully, tax-free. This is not the case with other savings accounts. The main advantage of a *Livret A* is that people feel it is safe, mainly because their parents probably had one. Also, it is really easy to open and often comes with a cash card for easy withdrawals.

Marianne If you go into the Mairie of any French town or village, you will spot a bust of an attractive woman in a prominent position on a plinth or on the wall above the Maire's desk. This is *Marianne* – symbol not so much of France but of the French

Republic. She was created by a sculptor called Injalbert and first started to appear in Mairies on the centenary of the French Revolution in 1889. *Marianne* is invariably represented wearing the woollen cap that was worn by women during the Revolution and which is known as a 'bonnet phrygien'. Before the introduction of the euro, you saw *Marianne* far more often: she was depicted on the back of the 1 franc and 5 franc coins as well as on all the old PIÈCES JAUNES. Nowadays you see her only as a stylized image on French postage stamps. In order to keep her as contemporary as possible, and to maintain public fervour, new busts are regularly produced based on whichever beautiful French woman is currently in the public eye. Recent *Mariannes* have been modelled on Brigitte Bardot, Catherine Deneuve and Laetitia Casta. The more recent the bust, the bustier it seems to be!

SDF This stands for 'Sans Domicile Fixe' – of no fixed abode – and is the common term for a homeless person. People refer to 'un *SDF*' and can be heard observing, for example, that 'Il y avait un *SDF* dans le train ce matin.' Using the full name, rather than the letters, can lead to misunderstandings. One winter four of these unfortunates froze to death in the streets in Paris. The news bulletin referred to the death of 'quatre sans domicile fixe', which several people, including me, misheard as 'quatre cents...', therefore assuming that four hundred people had died! If they should take to begging, a homeless person transforms from an *SDF* into 'un mendiant'.

The Calendar Year

People don't come to France just for the summer holidays any more: visitors now seem to take week-end breaks all the year round. With this in mind, I have set out words that relate to things that happen on various days of the week, as well as throughout the year. The Christmas and New Year period in particular has events and traditions with no equivalent in the UK. For example, how many presents do you receive from your family apart from on your birthday and at Christmas?

You will also see why you shouldn't worry if the air-raid sirens suddenly go off (assuming you are on holiday on a Wednesday) and find out which day you should try to be in France if you want to increase your chances of being kissed on the cheeks.

Midi/le Midi This is a commonly used term for a time of day that, according to certain people, does not actually exist. In French, a day can be broken down into 'le matin' or 'la matinée' (the morning), 'l'après-midi' (the afternoon), rounding off with 'le soir' or 'la soirée' (the evening). Many people use the term 'le *midi*' for lunchtime; purists, however, will have none of this and maintain that there is no such expression as 'le *midi*', believing that anything that happens around midday happens '*à midi*'. Some people will make an appointment to do something 'le *midi*', while others will meet up '*à midi*'. Those who say 'le *midi*' are also the sort of people who say manger and will therefore issue invitations for lunch by saying, 'Si on mangeais ensemble ce *midi*.' Those who eschew 'le *midi*' will also have nothing to do with manger and have to be clearer, and more long-winded, about their invitation, saying something like, 'Si nous déjeunions ensemble aujourd'hui.' The 'le *midi*' camp has a distinct advantage in that its term covers any time from around twelve to just after two. If whatever it is doesn't happen at precisely midday, the '*à midi*' lot has to use another expression, such as 'l'heure du déjeuner', which can be inconvenient. The main disadvantage of 'le *midi*' is when used as 'un *midi*' or one lunchtime. Unfortunately, this can be misheard as '*à midi*' and lead to disaster when a vague invitation to come to lunch one day – 'Si tu venais manger un *midi*' – is misheard as the definite 'Si tu venais manger à *midi*.'

The term *le Midi* is also a perfectly correct way of referring to the south of France, people spending their summer holidays 'dans *le Midi*'.

DAYS OF THE WEEK

Bonne fête This was a term I discovered on 4 November in the first year I lived in France. Arriving at work, I met my secretary in the corridor. Instead of her usual firm handshake and brief 'Bonjour, Charles. Ça va?', she greeted me cheerfully with, 'Ah! C'est votre fête aujourd'hui!' and kissed me soundly on both cheeks, exclaiming *'Bonne fête!'* In France, days of the year are associated with a given saint of the Roman Catholic Church and the names of the saints are the most frequently used French first names. For example, 10 September is the feast day of Sainte Inès and 4 November turns out to be the feast of Saint Charles. Most diaries and desk calendars show the name of the saint whose feast day or 'fête' is celebrated on each day of the year. When choosing names for children born in France you used to be allowed to pick only from those which figured on the calendar. Although this limited the choice, at least it spared children the embarrassment of being saddled with outrageous made-up names or being called after all the players of a football team. Not all days of the year have an associated saint's name. Some public holidays shown on the calendar are called by their title, such as 'Fête du travail' for the May Day holiday. There are tales of children of immigrants whose parents understood the principle of picking names from the calendar, but unfortunately picked 14 July as their inspiration, their poor kids being forced to grow up being called 'Fête Nat' or national holiday. A final, important point is that, if you are French, not only are you wished *bonne fête* on your feast day by members of your family, and kissed on the cheeks by all and sundry, but they also tend to give you a present. It is worth moving to France just for that!

Jour férié There are far more public holidays – *jours fériés* – in France than in the UK. It is a simple matter to check the list printed in diaries showing the dates of the various public holidays in countries around the world. According to my diary, whereas in the UK the number of public holidays is nine, France enjoys fourteen. Only Switzerland, with eighteen, has more. All French public holidays fall on their particular date and not always on a Monday as bank holidays do in the UK. This means that a given public holiday falls on a different weekday each year and leads to the creation of long weekends – see PONT. As for the nature of the holidays themselves, they generally have equivalents in the UK. Two of the historical ones, 11 November and 8 May, commemorate the end of respectively the First and the Second World Wars but are not celebrated as holidays in the UK. Other holidays are Catholic feast days. For example, Ascension and Assumption celebrate the ascension to heaven respectively of Jesus and Mary; and La TOUSSAINT is All Saints' Day.

Mercredi *Mercredi*, which, as I am sure you know, means Wednesday, is the day of the week when cinema programmes change. This is something to be aware of, if, like me, you come from a country where films used to change on a Sunday. As the new movies come out then, Wednesday is also the day that magazines such as *Pariscope* are published. *Pariscope* is the most popular of the various publications that give the details of cinema programmes in the Paris area, as well as information on theatres and museums. An established Parisian tradition consists of buying

Pariscope each week, studying it, marking the various films, exhibitions and plays that you plan to see that week, and then not actually getting round to seeing them. This is great fun, and particularly good value as *Pariscope* costs only 40c. *Mercredi* is also the most popular day of the week with young French schoolchildren because it is traditionally the day when there is no school, especially for those who have classes on Saturday morning. Finally, the first Wednesday of every month is special because at twelve noon on the dot all the sirens are tested. For a whole minute (which is a really long time when you are subjected to a Second World War air-raid siren just outside your window, as I am), the sirens wail their warning. Then, just as you've recovered your concentration, ten minutes later they sound the all-clear for thirty seconds.

THE YEAR

Cartes de vœux These are greetings cards, specifically those you send to friends at Christmas. In the UK it is traditional to make every effort to send your Christmas cards early enough to be sure that they are received before Christmas Day. Indeed, if cards arrive after Christmas, Brits assume that the sender had either forgotten them or only posted the card in reply to the one they received. In France, you don't have to rush because they are not considered Christmas cards at all. They are seen instead as New Year cards. As you are wishing people a Happy New Year, there is no point sending your card before the end of December. Most French people believe that they can be sent at any time up to the end of January. Unfortunately, in French offices, they tend to apply this principle to greetings cards sent to UK associates. I have tried several times to instill a sense of urgency into the posting of cards to the UK by my colleagues, but with no real success.

Étrennes Some people have all the luck. In certain, essentially Catholic, French families, you not only get a present on your birthday, at Christmas and on the day of your 'fête' – see BONNE FÊTE – you also get one for your *étrennes*. This is a small New Year's present that is typically given only by immediate family to their children or grandchildren. Nevertheless, when I first met someone around New Year who was brandishing the present that he had had for his *étrennes*, I confess that I felt a bit jealous. This guy got presents on twice as many occasions a year as me!

However, the more common sense of *étrennes* is Christmas box. In the weeks before Christmas a seemingly endless procession of people will ring your doorbell and expect to be given a small financial gift to mark the festive period. This will include some or all of the following: the postman, the dustmen, the local firemen, the local policemen and the road menders, known as 'les cantonniers'. Some will give you a receipt, supposedly so that you can set the sum off against the following year's taxes. Others will give you a Christmas card with a festive message and a calendar. The more generous will stretch to a proper calendar, usually bearing a large, brightly coloured photo of a kitten. Experience shows that in late November it is a good idea to prepare an envelope and leave it near the front door with appropriate sums of cash ready, as well as a pen to make a list of who calls. Second visits, whether intentional or not, are not uncommon and should be rebuffed with a firm 'Mais, vous êtes déjà venus.' Certain miserly householders are rumoured to try this on the first call!

Noël When, in my twenty-second year, I set out to spend my first Christmas in France, I was prepared for many things to be completely different. I had, however, somehow assumed that Christmas would at least be celebrated on the same date as in the UK. This assumption proved to be misguided as the Christmas meal – see RÉVEILLON – took place on the evening of 24 December. Cautious enquiries about exchanging presents led to more surprises. This was to happen at the end of the meal, around midnight. Further questions about a possible substantial lunch on the 25th were met with incomprehension. Nothing was planned for the 25th at all! I have since discovered that there are numerous French families who give their presents on Christmas morning, but nevertheless still have their Christmas feast on the previous evening. My first Christmas Day in France with no huge meal, no presents, not even a James Bond film on TV, was a sorry affair indeed.

Paquet cadeau This term, which literally means present package is the French for gift wrap. It is a splendid aspect of French culture and is something that I never imagined existed until the day I went to buy some perfume for my wife. Once I had ordered what I wanted, the salesgirl enquired, 'C'est pour offrir?', wanting to know if the perfume was intended as a gift for someone. Wondering what business it was of hers, I mumbled something indistinct, whereupon the girl set about wrapping the perfume in expensive paper, lengths of ribbon and sticky gold labels. The resulting package was a masterpiece. And there was no extra charge. Gift-wrapping is part of the service. In the run-up to Christmas, most French shops gift wrap more or less automatically. There are often special counters after the cash registers where the girls do nothing but gift wrap. It is traditional to tip them, provided they make a good job of it. If the shops are too big, or too busy, to gift wrap, they provide sheets of branded wrapping paper or colourful envelopes for customers to take away with their purchases so that they can wrap them at home. The only problem is that the person receiving the present will spot straight away where you bought it, and try to guess what it might be.

Réveillon A key word to learn if you are going to be in France over Christmas and the New Year. The French mostly celebrate NOËL with a huge Christmas meal on the evening of 24 December and this occasion is known as 'le *réveillon*'. People leave the office early on the afternoon of the 24th saying things like, 'On va fêter le *réveillon* chez mes parents' and head off to the station. There is also a verb, 'réveillonner', which quite logically means having a big meal on 24 December. However, things never being simple, the word *réveillon* is disconcertingly ambiguous. As well as referring to the Christmas meal of 24 December, the term applies to the feast that is eaten on New Year's Eve. No family's New Year's Eve celebration would be complete, or even possible, without at least a four-course meal, including some or all of the following: oysters, foie gras, smoked salmon, a roast of some sort, a selection of cheeses, a chocolate dessert and plenty of wine. Champagne, of course, is served at the stroke of midnight.

The generic expression for Christmas and New Year's Eve together is 'les fêtes'. For example, people agree to meet up in January 'après les fêtes'.

Toussaint This is the day of the year when everybody remembers the dead. When you visit a cemetery in the UK on any given day, you are likely to see one or two graves with recent flowers, several graves with faded or fading blooms and the majority with nothing at all. This is because most people tend to lay flowers on their relatives' graves only on the anniversary of their death or on some other occasion such as a birthday. In France, as well as visiting their relatives' graves in the course of the year, people will, almost without exception, also do so on 'La *Toussaint*'. Thus, 1 November is a day notorious for the volume of traffic on the roads, and sadly the number of road accidents, as people travel to lay flowers on family graves. Tradition has it that only certain flowers are suitable. Basically, you can choose between carnations and chrysanthemums. Florists all over France stock up on these varieties in the last days of October each year so as to be ready for the rush and despite the fact that 1 November is a public holiday, most florists will be open, at least in the morning. The graveyard which slopes up the hill behind our local church is quite crowded from mid-morning onwards on 'La *Toussaint*', mostly with family groups who come to lay new flowers and tidy the graves.

ANNUAL EVENTS

Pièces jaunes Before the arrival of the euro, French coins included the 5 franc, 2 franc, 1 franc and 50 centimes coins, all of which were shiny silver-coloured. The remaining coins, those of lesser value, the 20, 10 and 5 centimes, were made of golden-coloured alloy and were known as 'les *pièces jaunes*'. Desperate beggars would encourage you to give them any amount, however small, with the words 'J'accepte même les *pièces jaunes*.' There is a traditional annual event, known as 'Opération *pièces jaunes*', which was started in 1989 and headed by the then President's wife, Bernadette Chirac, to raise money for children's hospitals. Decorated cardboard charity boxes are placed in public buildings, post offices and schools and people are encouraged to put in their spare change, while well-publicized trains travel the length and breadth of France collecting literally tons of coins. Euro coins also include *pièces jaunes* but their value is considerably higher than their old franc counterparts.

Signes du zodiaque

The signs of the zodiac are another source of confusion when you start learning French. As all the names of the signs appear to be classical in origin, I had assumed that they would be roughly similar in French. In fact, only one, Cancer, is exactly the same in both languages. Some of them are close, such as Capricorne, Sagittaire, Taureau, Lion, Gémeaux and Scorpion. But poor Libra, Pisces, Aries and Aquarius are unrecognizable, becoming respectively Balance (because of the scales), Poissons, Bélier and Verseau. Luckily, horoscopes in French newspapers include the dates to which the signs apply so that you can quickly track down the right one. Virgo gets a special mention because in French it is 'Vierge', which means virgin. Asking Virgo people what sign they are is particularly entertaining because they have to answer 'Je suis Vierge' – I am a virgin – and may even blush.

How to Sound French

I have to admit that the title of this section is, perhaps, a little optimistic. For a start, I know all the words and no one has ever suggested that I sound French. What is more, I have no reason to assume that you actually want to sound French. Nevertheless, I have always believed it is better to aim higher rather than lower. So, even if you don't end up being taken for a French person, this selection of words should at least help you to stand out from the run-of-the-mill crowd of tourists. And that is probably achievement enough for many of us.

But back to the words. They cover such a broad range of subjects that they haven't been grouped together but are simply set out in alphabetical order. You will find here words that don't mean quite what they seem, words that cause problems even to the French and a couple of English Christian names that might be misconstrued in France.

Brave There are two French adjectives – the other is GENTIL – that at first sight seem to mean something kind and friendly, but which in fact have the opposite meaning. At school you learn that *brave* means courageous, gallant or just plain brave. However, you hear individuals who are clearly neither brave nor gallant, even less courageous, being described as 'Il est *brave*' or 'C'est un *brave* homme' by people who are obviously not intending to be flattering. The clue is in the tone of voice, which is usually insulting or at least patronizing. 'Il est *brave*' means roughly that he is a nice enough fellow, basically harmless, but that you shouldn't expect too much from him. I had a colleague, who could best be described as wishy-washy, of whom all that my other colleagues could say was that 'Il est *brave*' in a sneery voice while shaking their heads sadly. It seems to be most often applied to men.

Certain An odd word in that its meaning changes according to whether you stick it before or after a noun. If you put the adjective before the noun, it adds a notion of vagueness to whatever it is; if you put it after the noun, things become much more definite. For example, an elderly person could be described as being of 'un *certain* âge', which means they are quite old but could still be expected to get full value from a new magazine subscription, while saying that they are of 'un âge *certain*' means that they are really old and decrepit. You can echo a phrase that someone has said including the word *certain* but reverse its position to add emphasis. For example, when something has been causing you problems you might say 'J'ai connu une *certaine* difficulté,' whereupon the person you are talking to responds 'Ou une difficulté *certaine*' and smiles knowingly to show that the difficulty that you were faced with was tougher than you are letting on.

Chambre/salon

'Une *chambre*', as you undoubtedly learned at school, means a bedroom. However, you quite often hear people saying that they spent the weekend going round the furniture shops to buy 'une nouvelle *chambre*'. Visions arise of them coming home in a big truck with an extra room that they somehow manage to add on to the structure of their house. In fact, 'une *chambre*' in this context means a collection of matching bedroom furniture, typically all bought at once in the same shop. Should it be for a child's room, when the kid grows out of it you can advertise it as 'une *chambre* d'enfant' in the second-hand section of newspapers. The only detail provided will be the style, probably 'pin' or pine, or, my pet hate, 'rustique moderne', a vile term which really means that the furniture is cheap, badly made and has a fake, vaguely country-antique look about it.

The word *salon*, which means living room, can similarly be applied to a collection of furniture suitable for such a room. Some people try to make their furniture sound even more chic by calling it 'un living' instead of 'un *salon*'. Both are words you should understand if you hear them, but never say.

Chez

You would not believe the problems that can be caused by this short word. It means simply at or to. You probably know that our house is '*chez* nous'. Similarly, people who are going home say, 'Je vais rentrer *chez* moi' and there is nothing wrong with that. Problems arise, not when people say *chez* but when another word is used instead. Going to the dentist, the doctor or the hairdresser should be described by using the word '*chez*' as in 'Je vais *chez* le médecin' or 'Je suis allé *chez* le coiffeur.' Unfortunately, some people use 'au' instead of *chez* and say, though it causes me real pain to write this, 'Je suis allé *au* coiffeur' or 'Je vais *au* dentiste.' It's worse than having your teeth drilled!

Condamné This word means sentenced or condemned. However, confusingly, you often see signs on doors which read: 'Porte *condamnée*'. When I saw one of these for the first time I wondered what the poor door had done to be punished like that. In fact *condamnée* in this context means blocked off or sealed off and the sign is there to stop you wasting your time shaking the door handle and vainly trying to open it.

Couvent/couvent These two words, which look identical, are included as examples of the duplicity of French pronunciation. In fairness, the majority of French words are pronounced as you would expect, but *couvent* is a nice example of a word that is pronounced differently according to its meaning. When it is a verb – the third person plural of the present of 'couver', which is the act of sitting on its eggs by a hen (or other bird) – it is pronounced 'coove'. *Couvent*, however, can also be a noun meaning nunnery or convent. In this case it is pronounced 'coove-en'. Hens laying in a convent would be translated as 'Les poules *couvent* dans le *couvent*', with the identical words being pronounced quite differently. This is about as hard as pronunciation gets in French, but, it must be admitted, is kids' stuff compared to slough, cough, bough, chough, through and though, which together can make foreign students give up and leave the UK for ever.

Cucul If you happen to know that the word 'cul' is particularly rude and means arse, you may fear the worst when you first hear someone described as being *cucul*. In fact, it is a fairly innocent slang word that means wishy-washy or wet in the schoolboy sense. An uninteresting, rather prim and fussy girl, the sort you definitely wouldn't flirt with at a party, may be described as *cucul* or, inexplicably, as '*cucul* la praline' ('praline' usually means a crunchy, sugared almond sweet). *Cucul* is not an adjective that you want to hear used of one of your friends or relatives.

D'accord An omnipresent word. Indeed, most French people would be incapable of having a discussion without it. The expression 'être *d'accord*' means to agree. Of course, people don't say 'Je suis *d'accord*' any more than Brits say 'I agree with you.' They shorten it to *d'accord* in the way others say 'OK'. When someone is on the phone setting up an appointment, you will hear *d'accord* increasingly often as the two people reach agreement on what they are going to do, where and when and the conversation draws to its end, usually marked by a decisive 'Ça marche!' – that's fine. Of course, using the final 'Ça marche!' does not preclude using *d'accord* a couple more times afterwards, just to tidy things up. There are those who think that *d'accord* itself is too long and shorten it further to 'd'acc'. The opposite of 'Je suis *d'accord*' is 'Je ne suis pas *d'accord*.' This is rarely shortened to 'pas *d'accord*', except when presenting a debate, summing up the opposing positions as '*d'accord*' and 'pas *d'accord*'. If you get fed up with saying *d'accord* more than twenty times in a long conversation, you can always vary things a bit by using 'entendu' – understood – a few times.

De The possessive form – when you want to make clear that something belongs to someone – should be *de* in French. The famous first phrase that you were supposed to learn at school was 'la plume *de* ma tante'. In general terms, therefore, the thing belonging to someone is 'le truc *de* quelqu'un'. Unfortunately, not everyone says *de*; a fair number of people say 'à' – for example, 'la voiture *à* Paul' rather than 'la voiture *de* Paul'. This is a heinous error and should be avoided at all costs because you really don't want to sound like the sort of person who makes this kind of mistake. The only time you are allowed to say 'à' instead of *de* is when you are blaming someone. In *Les Misérables* by Victor Hugo, Gavroche says: 'C'est la faute à Rousseau . . . c'est la faute à Voltaire.' Victor Hugo, of course, knew it was a mistake. If you are imitating Gavroche and say something like 'Ce n'était pas moi: c'est la faute à Pierre,' this is OK because it is clear what you are doing. However, some people use 'à' instead of *de* for all sorts of things and, when you remonstrate with them, try to justify themselves by referring to Gavroche. Do not be fooled: they really are making a mistake.

Dont/que Take heart! You are not alone. French people make mistakes too when speaking or writing French. One of the most common is putting *que* where they should put *dont*. As a general rule, *dont* takes the place of 'de quoi' and is used with verbs that are followed by '*de*' such as 'se souvenir de' for remember. There are several common expressions which require the use of *dont*; for example, when being scared of something. This is 'avoir peur de quelque chose'. But when you turn it around to say, 'What I'm scared of . . .', it should become 'Ce *dont* j'ai peur . . .' Unfortunately, certain people (and it is always the same people as in other examples in this book) say, 'Ce *que* j'ai peur . . .' This is quite simply appalling. Should you hear someone say this, or 'Ce *que* je me souviens' instead of 'Ce *dont* je me souviens', feel free to berate them most forcefully. The fact that this comes from a foreigner might just shame them into changing their erroneous ways.

En revanche I include this not because it is particularly interesting but because it was one of my first boss's pet obsessions. There are two ways of saying on the other hand in French. One is the more commonly used 'par contre', the other is *en revanche*. Purists heap scorn on 'par contre', accusing it of being semantically incorrect and common. Others believe that there are certain, clearly defined contexts where you should use one or the other expression. Unfortunately, when questioned, they can never explain what these circumstances actually are. Nevertheless, after working in an environment where 'par contre' was more or less forbidden on pain of receiving an irritating reprimand, I have for ever forsaken it and only ever say *en revanche*. Feel free to use whichever one you choose, but you can't go wrong if you always say *en revanche*.

Espace This is an easy one: if in doubt, stick the word *espace* at the beginning of whatever it is. It is the word that is really 'à la mode' or fashionable. *Espace* means space or room but, over the past decade, it has come to be used to try to make practically anything sound smarter and more trendy. The meeting room at work has been refurbished and is no longer known as 'la salle de réunion'; it has a bright new label on the door that reads '*espace* réunion'. Similarly, what used to be a 'zone fumeurs' or smoking area, is now an '*espace* fumeurs'. But using *espace* to make everything sound modern, cool and up to date doesn't always work; for example, when the grubby office corridor with the coffee machine was relabelled '*espace* café'. And the word infiltrates everything: the meeting hall of the village where we live is now referred to as 'l'*espace* culturel' or culture space. It still feels just like a village hall, though.

Foie/foi/fois/Foix Four words that sound exactly the same. The first means liver, the next one means faith, the third is time and the last is a place name. When you hear someone exclaim 'Ma *foi*!' you can deduce that he is talking about his faith and not his liver because *foi* is feminine while *foie* is masculine. Not to mention the fact that an exclamation about one's liver would be odd, even for a French person!

I learned a poem at school designed to help you remember which is which. It goes:

> Il était une fois
> Un homme de foi
> Qui mangeait du foie
> Dans la ville de Foix
>
> Il se dit 'Ma foi!
> C'est la première fois
> Et la dernière fois
> Que je mange du foie
> Dans la ville de Foix.'

Gare! *Gare!* with an exclamation mark after it has nothing to do with *gare* without one. You probably know that 'une *gare*' is a railway station – in my O Level French textbook, people spent an inordinate amount of time asking the way to the nearest one. Knowing this, I was perplexed to read a newspaper headline which proclaimed: '*Gare* aux explosions!' because it seemed to have nothing to do with stations. *Gare!* means watch out and comes from the verb 'se garer', which usually means to park your car but in this context means to watch out for, or to avoid something. A painter would urge you to mind the wet paint by saying, '*Gare* à la peinture!', while an irritable parent would tell a young child to do something and back it up with a threat to '*Gare* à toi!' if they don't, or, worse, '*Gare* à tes fesses!', warning them to watch out for a smack. You might think that you should say 'garez!' to someone you say 'vous' to, but *gare!* is an interjection not an imperative, so you don't. If you do something spontaneously, or without warning, you do it 'Sans crier *gare!*'

Gentil This is the other of the two French adjectives (see BRAVE) that, while it can be meant in a friendly, flattering way, can also be somewhat less complimentary. In its polite sense, it means kind or nice. You can thank someone by saying, 'Merci. Vous êtes très *gentil*,' or observe some act of kindness with the words 'C'est *gentil*' and no one will take offence. You can even compliment someone on their charming home by remarking, 'C'est *gentil* chez vous,' but I wouldn't necessarily want anyone to say that about our house. Where things start to go downhill is when you say of someone – and of course never to their face – 'Il est très *gentil*, mais . . .' or simply 'Il est *gentil* . . .' in a sarcastic tone, with a sneer on your face. Said like that, *gentil* conveys the meaning that he is a nice enough person, I suppose, but that is really all that can be said about him. Quite a lot for such a short simple word.

Glace sans tain I had to include this notably because it was only when checking in a dictionary that I discovered that it is *tain* and not 'teint' as I had long assumed. In truth, I find the French phrase and the corresponding English one equally annoying as neither description is accurate. The British call this a two-way mirror, but that is exactly what it isn't. You can see through it only from one side; you can't see through the other at all because it is shiny. If you could see through it both ways, there wouldn't be much point in having it and it would be called a window. The French version is annoying because it means mirror without silvering, but the mirror *does* have silvering, or rather the modern equivalent of it. If it didn't, it wouldn't look like a mirror from the side you can't see through. I feel much better for sharing this with you! Thank you.

H The letter *H* is a tricky one in French, especially when it comes at the beginning of a word. For once a word starts with an *H*, the problem of elision raises its ugly head. Elision, the carrying over of the sound from the end of one word into the start of the next is a perennial French problem. If you are faced with the words 'les haricots', you have to decide whether you should say something like 'lay aricots' or whether you can be sloppy and get away with 'lez aricots' with the s of 'les' sliding into the beginning of 'haricots'. In this example, you quite definitely have to make the effort to go for the 'lay aricots' version. This is specified clearly in all the books and backed up by the Académie Française and you don't want to get on the wrong side of them. In the better dictionaries, the phonetic spelling of the word has a little apostrophe before it to show that you have to say 'lay' and not 'lez'. Other words such as 'hôtel' are the opposite. Saying 'lay hôtels' sounds silly. You are free, indeed are encouraged, to say 'lez hôtels'. Occasionally, a French person may stop in mid-sentence and enquire, 'Est-ce que l'on dit lez hirondelles ou lay hirondelles?', which usually leads to collective disagreement and the person forgetting the original question. In some cases the debate becomes very tricky indeed. There are words where elision used not to be allowed but about which, inexplicably, the Académie Française has had a change of heart and now allows it. There are even words about which the Académie can't make up its mind and just suggests that elision might be allowable but is really frowned upon in the best circles. An example of this is the word 'handicappés'.

Haro I include this word because I once sparked off a fairly acrimonious dispute between two complete strangers sitting either side of me on a plane simply by asking what it meant. It was in a headline on the front page of a paper which read simply: '*Haro* sur le gaspillage'. The 'gaspillage' bit was OK; I knew that it meant wastage. The *haro* part caused problems. One passenger claimed that it was a cry for help in case of robbery, when any person hearing it became entitled to arrest the perpetrator. This turns out to be true, but it wasn't the sense in which it was used in the article. The other claimed that crying *haro* was a sign of reproach or condemnation of the thing in question. This seemed to fit the headline better. Inexplicably, both of them kept saying '*haro* sur le baudet' – a 'baudet' being a sort of donkey. To my frustration though, neither of them could explain what that expression meant nor, more interestingly, why they both knew it.

Invariable Just when you start to get the hang of French, you come across the hurdle of 'les mots *invariables*'. Practically every

French word acquires an s on the end in the plural – apart from the ones that take an x, like 'chou' or 'cadeau'. There are exceptions to most rules and the exceptions in this case are 'les mots *invariables*', words whose singular and plural forms are the same. It must be said that there aren't many of them, and, what's more, they are not things that you talk about all that often. For example, there is the word for lampshade, 'abat-jour'. If you have one it is 'un abat-jour' and if you are lucky enough to have three it is 'trois abat-jour'. Similarly, one windscreen is 'un pare-brise', while two cars between them have 'deux pare-brise'. But, since both singular and plural forms sound the same, if you say the words, rather than write them, no one will know whether you are aware that you are dealing with such 'mots *invariables*'. Unfortunately, now that you do know about them, no one will realize that either.

-**Marie** Very few English men are called Mary. Similarly, *Marie* is mainly a girl's name in France, whether alone or in compound, such as *Marie*-Claire or *Marie*-Béatrice. But, strange as it may seem, it can also appear in male compound names. You have only to think of M. Le Pen, whose Christian name is Jean-*Marie*. If anyone thinks ill of him, it probably isn't on account of his name. You'll also come across men called Pierre-*Marie* or Paul-*Marie*. Such names usually crop up in particularly devout Catholic families. When I first encountered a Jean-*Marie*, I thought it was hilarious that the poor bloke was called Mary. Unfortunately, no one else seemed to think it was odd at all, so I laughed alone. While it is fairly common for men to have compound names ending with *Marie*, no male has a name beginning with it: this is reserved for women. On the other hand, men do suffer the indignity of having compound names that begin with Ange, or angel. I recently met an

Ange-Dominique and was much amused by the name. Again, I laughed alone, because it is apparently a typical Corsican name, and you really don't want to upset a Corsican. Finally, you can combine *Marie* and Ange to make the woman's name *Marie*-Ange. Perhaps this is indicative of coming from a devout Corsican Catholic family.

On You could probably write a whole book just about this single short word. Its uses are numerous and its strength can be surprising. At its simplest level *on* means one or someone. An unknown person punching you in the street would be described as '*On* m'a frappé.' More commonly *on* means us, in that it takes the place of the word NOUS in sentences such as '*On* est allé au restaurant.' If this statement is given in answer to a question addressed to a couple along the lines of 'What did you do this weekend?', it is clear that the *on* refers to the two members of the couple. However, *on* can be used to preserve secrets or to avoid divulging information. The same question, 'What did you do this weekend?', addressed to someone who doesn't speak about their personal relationships, will lead to exactly the same answer: '*On* est allé au restaurant,' but this time the *on* can mean absolutely anything from the entire French Olympic weightlifting team and I, to my secret lover and I, to the more mundane my parents took me out to lunch but I don't want to admit to it. The word *on* can be used to give instructions to someone while making it clear that it doesn't much matter who does it; the only important point is that it won't be the person giving the orders. Discussing the need to write a letter, my current boss will say in his particular fashion, 'Il faut qu'*on* écrive une lettre.' This means that someone has to do it, but it clearly won't be him. If there are two or more people involved, no one will know who should be preparing the letter, even though everyone will know who won't be doing it. You can also use *on* to claim unde-served credit for something done by others. By saying 'On a obtenu un contrat très important,' you can try to imply that you were involved in the negotiation of the contract, even though you were on holiday at the time. Fortunately, this tactic rarely works.

Paf, pan, plouf Learning a foreign language is a long and exhausting business. Not only do you have a huge number of words to master, you also have to learn the various onomatopoeic sounds for everyday events. By this, I mean words like splash, bang, crunch that are used to represent what kind of sound occurred. You only have to look at an Astérix cartoon book to see that all the sound words are different in French. Someone falling into water goes splash in the UK; in France, they will get just as wet but will go *plouf*. Being hit in the face with a large fish sounds like *paf* in French, where it would be smash in English. Slamming into some-thing produces 'vlan' instead of slam, while a short sharp hitting sound is 'poc'. A quick look at any episode of *Tintin* shows that French guns don't go bang but, rather pathetically, *pan*.

There is also a wonderful word for falling over and hurting yourself which is 'badaboum!' Small children tell you they have fallen down by saying, 'J'ai fait badaboum!', while parents, observ-ing their offspring smack into the tarmac, will say helpfully, 'Oh! Badaboum!', as though the child might not have noticed that they have just fallen over.

Finally, it is as well to know that when you have been struck by something which goes *paf*, you should cry out 'Aïe!' rather than 'Ouch!' or no one will come and comfort you.

Pas évident The word 'évident' means obvious or clear, but seems to be used more often in the negative as *pas évident*. While this literally means not obvious, the term implies that whatever particular task we are talking about is particularly tricky and should be expected to cause some difficulty when you come to dealing with it. Asking a plumber whether he can fix something will lead to much sucking in of breath and a discouraging 'C'est *pas évident*.' This, of course, doesn't mean that he won't be able to fix it. Rather it is intended to make you understand how grateful you will be expected to be once he has done so. It is not only the person faced with the task who is allowed to say, 'C'est *pas évident*.' Any pessimistic bystander or spectator will invariably dampen your enthusiasm for the job in hand with a shake of the head accompanied by a despondent 'C'est *pas évident*.' Such people even seem disappointed when you manage to accomplish the task.

Pavillon One of the first French words you learn is that for house, which is 'maison'. But it turns out that there are far fewer 'maisons' in France than might be supposed. What there are lots of are *pavillons*. Though this word looks as though it might mean pavilion and imply something rather grand, it is in fact just the common word for a small, modern house set in a bit of garden and sitting between two other identical houses. A series of *pavillons* together is 'une zone pavillonnaire'. Somehow, therefore, the word *pavillon* is less flattering than 'maison'. I always refer to the family home as 'notre maison' and try never to use the word *pavillon* at all. When you have something delivered, the man in the shop always asks, 'Vous êtes en appartement ou en pavillon?' in order to have some idea of how many steps and other obstacles may be encountered. I resolutely reply, 'En maison.' Young married couples in

France dream of moving into a brand-new *pavillon* that they have just had built, more or less to order. During the period when the *pavillon* is under construction, they will proudly boast to all and sundry that 'On est en train de faire construire.' The fact that what is being built is a *pavillon* is so obvious that the word doesn't even need to be mentioned.

Péter It is not necessarily a good idea to go and live in France if your first name happens to be Peter. For *péter*, albeit with an accent, means to fart. A fart is 'un pet', a word that I once managed to confuse with 'une pie' – a magpie – thus bringing about a shocked, collective silence at a christening party, for Monet did not paint any pictures of farts. The verb *péter* is quite handy as it can be used for a broader range of things than just passing wind. The explosion of bombs and other noisy devices is described as *péter*, as are the bursting of zips and the splitting of seams. Busting pretty much anything, from a vase to your nose, can also be vividly rendered as 'Je l'ai pété.' But its scope is broader still. If you drink too much, you can be described as being '*pété*', somewhat in the way that you would use the word pissed. You can draw a parallel between this expression and the English pissed as a fart. Finally, you can even make up compound words like 'pète-sec', which, rather than having anything to do with farts, defines someone who is bossy and sharp-tongued.

Incidentally, there are girls' names, too, that may cause misunderstandings in France, notably Penny. Penny sounds uncomfortably similar to the word 'pénis', which means exactly what it looks as though it means.

Petit You could probably write a thesis on the use of the word *petit*. In its basic sense it means little as opposed to big. But what is much more interesting is the way that it is used to encourage someone to accept something. To understand what I mean, just go to any restaurant in France. Whenever the waiter suggests that you might like to have anything over and above the basic minimum, he will define whatever it is as being *petit*. At the beginning of the meal, before you have ordered, he will ask if you want a drink. But he won't say, 'Voulez-vous un apéritif?', he will say, 'Voulez-vous un *petit* apéritif?' By doing so, he will suggest that it is not unreasonable, nor in any way extravagant, to order one, and that no one will think any the worse of you if you do. There will then be silence on the *petit* front until the end of the main course, whereupon the waiter will enquire, 'Un *petit* dessert?' Of course you will have a '*petit* dessert' – being *petit* it can't be too fattening or too expensive, and the kind waiter is merely doing you a favour by reminding you of this. After you have finished your pudding, the friendly waiter will use the word one last time by suggesting 'un *petit* café'. I have never been offered just 'un café' in a restaurant, but when I have asked waiters why they use the word *petit* like this, none of them admits to doing it consciously. You can also use the word *petit* at home to announce the wine that you are going to serve to your guests at a meal. By calling it 'un *petit* vin' you make it clear that it is not a hugely expensive, famous-name affair, but rather a modest, though good-quality wine that you have selected specially for their consumption.

Photographe This is one of the dirtier tricks that the French language comes up with to upset foreigners. If you were faced with the term 'un *photographe*', what would you think it meant? I imagine that you would assume, like I did, that it was French for a photo. But no! It is French for a photographer. If you say, as I once did, 'Il y a beaucoup de *photographes* dans mon album,' people will be most surprised and wonder how on earth you manage to carry it around. The correct word for a photo is 'une photographie'. This is generally shortened to 'une photo'. There is another common word for photo which also causes confusion among foreigners – 'un cliché'. If someone offers to show you their 'clichés', I don't know what you might imagine but it probably wouldn't be holiday snaps.

Qu'à cela ne tienne I include this for the simple reason that when I heard it the first few times, I was convinced that it was a single word. My colleagues used to pronounce it so fast that it was impossible to identify any of its constituent parts. For quite some time I thought that one bit of it was 'Aslan' and that they were invoking some fictional deity. In fact, as you can see, it is several words, put together in a way that makes their meaning impossible to guess. I'm still not sure what the expression literally means in French. In English, though, it comes out as no problem or even, in some circumstances, so be it.

Radio Of all the French words that you have to learn, the easiest are those beginning with X – they are the ones most likely to be exactly the same in both languages. Take, for example, xenon, xenophobe or xylophone. They are all, give or take an accent, the same in both. There are two main exceptions. One is the drink sherry, which is 'xérès' in French. The other came to light when I heard someone say that they were off to Paris 'pour une *radio*'. When they later returned empty-handed, I expressed commiseration that their shopping trip had been unsuccessful. However, my commiseration turned out to have been misplaced because the *radio* in question was not the transistor device which enables you to listen to *The Archers*. My colleague had in fact gone for an X-ray. *Radio* is short for 'radiographie'. The rays themselves are 'rayons X'.

Rhume 'Avoir un *rhume*' is to have a cold. However, French people, or possibly just Parisians, rarely seem to use the word, apparently believing that it doesn't sound serious enough. They tend to go to their GP and return proudly announcing that of course it wasn't a cold but that they are suffering from 'une rhinite', 'une trachéite' or, better still, something with a long and impressive-sounding name like 'une rhinopharyngite'. The longer the name given to the complaint, the longer the illness seems to last and the longer and louder the patient complains about it. Being sublimely indifferent to the fact that, whatever you call it, the illness is of viral origin and thus completely immune to antibiotics, the sufferer will loudly consume 'mes antibiotiques' at mealtimes. Speaking from painful experience, it is not a good idea to try to point out to someone that their antibiotics will in no way act on their viral infection. You run the risk of a sharp reply such as 'Alors, tu en connais plus que mon médecin?' – so you think you know more about it than my doctor?

Scotch Yet another source of confusion! The word *Scotch* used by a French person usually refers not to whisky but to transparent adhesive tape, which is not sold under the Sellotape brand as it is in the UK, but carries the name of its French manufacturer, Scotch. I still remember the first time a colleague came into my office declaring, 'Je cherche du *Scotch*. Est-ce que tu en as?' and I wondered whether he had taken me for a closet alcoholic.

Scotch whisky, by the way, is known as 'du whisky'.

Si/si Two more words that sound the same but have quite different meanings. The simpler one of the two is if and doesn't require any further explanation. The other meaning of *si* has no direct equivalent in English. In French there are two degrees of yes words – an ordinary one, 'oui', and an emphatic one, *si*. In English, if someone phrases their question as a negative, for example, 'Didn't you enjoy the film?', the person has to make their reply more forceful by saying, 'Yes, I did' instead of just 'Yes.' Alternatively, if you accuse someone of not having done something, for example, 'You haven't finished your homework,' they may reply, 'Yes, I have.' In French, in answer to a negative question or an accusation, you use *si* rather than just 'oui'. Getting it wrong, for example replying to the question, 'Tu n'aimes pas le couscous?' with a simple 'Oui, oui' apparently sounds particularly odd to the French, who can't understand why the existence of two words for the same thing should cause anyone any problem.

Subjonctif The subjunctive form of verbs is used far more often in French than in English. What's more, while you can't really hear the difference in English, the subjunctive really stands out in French. For example, any instruction along the lines of let him do this or it is necessary that you go there needs the subjunctive in French (as it does in English). The problem is that some subjunctives don't look anything like the other forms of the verb. The present of 'savoir', for example, is 'je sais, tu sais' but becomes 'que je sache, que tu saches' in the present subjunctive (there are all sorts of strange tenses in the subjunctive). I actually searched for the verb 'sacher' – without success – in a dictionary when I was trying to figure out what 'que je sache' meant. 'Faire', while happily giving us 'je fais, tu fais' in the present, goes to 'que je fasse, que tu fasses' in the subjunctive, which is similarly confusing.

Système D. Another enlightening view of the French character, as seen by the French themselves. As well as believing that 'IMPOSS-IBLE n'est pas français,' they are convinced that one of their essential traits is their ability to find ingenious solutions to problems that would confound anyone else, i.e. those unfortunates who are not French. When faced with some conundrum, people say that they will have to resort to *système D.* to solve it. But what is this 'D.'? There is a verb starting with D, 'se débrouiller', that means to find a way round problems and you may innocently believe that this is the D in question. Not a bit of it. The truth is much more vulgar – 'se démerder', which literally means to get yourself out of the shit. This is why you use only the verb's initial. Those rare people who actually are good at sorting things out and making a go of it are referred to as 'démerde', and you may be pointed in the direction of one of them for help because 'Il est très démerde.'

Tapis The English word carpet can be used quite happily to describe both a fitted carpet and the sort of non-fitted carpet that could be considered a big rug. In French, the word *tapis* that you learn at school as the translation of carpet, in fact can only be applied to the non-fitted carpet, the kind of thing that North African rug sellers still hawk from door to door. A fitted carpet has its own name, 'moquette'. If you tell someone that you have 'une nouvelle moquette', they will immediately assume that it is fitted. There doesn't seem to be a word for rug. You have to call it 'un petit *tapis*'. By the way, under the Pont Alexandre III in Paris, there is a sign, now sadly painted over, which used to tell passers-by the one thing they were specifically forbidden from doing under the bridge – beat carpets!

Trente-trois Ask a Brit how old Christ was when he was cruci-fied and they very probably won't know. On the other hand, most French people know that he died at the age of thirty-three. This came to light on my thirty-third birthday, when practically all my colleagues, on finding out how old I was, declared, 'Ah! L'âge du Christ.' It is interesting to note that Christ is called 'le Christ' in France (which explains why it is 'l'âge *du* Christ' and not 'l'âge *de* Christ').

Trente-trois also crops up in a medical context. When a doctor asks to look at your throat in the UK, you typically say ahh! In France, for reasons that have never been satisfactorily explained, it used to be traditional to say *trente-trois*.

Tutoyer One of the main differences between French and Eng-lish, and one that makes life needlessly difficult for a foreigner, is the fact that the French have two common words for 'you'. While you can say thee and thou in English, you generally save them for when you are addressing God. For day-to-day use, you make do with you. In French you have the choice between 'vous', when you are addressing someone you don't know very well, or have a formal relationship with (see VOUVOYER), and 'tu', when you speak to friends and family. Discussing whether to say 'tu' or 'vous' to someone is such a common subject that the French have devised a handy verb, *tutoyer*, which means to say 'tu' to. And the practice of *tutoyer* is called 'tutoiement'.

Tuyau 'Un *tuyau*' is a length of pipe or tubing, the sort of thing that connects your tap to the water main. It is a useful term to know in the French world of it's not what you know but who you know because it means a helpful tip or hint which someone more knowledgeable is prepared to share with you. When revising for an exam, a friend may come up and say, with the pride of one who knows something interesting, 'J'ai un *tuyau* pour l'examen' before going on to tell you that he's found out from some source or other that there is going to be a question about Russian history. In this sense, it is privileged information, something that you shouldn't be entitled to have. You can also ask people, 'Vous avez des *tuyaux*?' about a confidential subject or about some practical task for which you need helpful advice. For 'un *tuyau*' also covers things like DIY or cookery. In fact, whatever the subject, you should expect to do better at it if someone gives you 'un *tuyau*'. If the advice turns out to be no good, the information becomes 'un *tuyau* crevé' or a burst pipe.

Version There are many English words that don't have a direct French translation and thus require a description in a dictionary. A simple example is pith. If you look it up, you'll find something like 'la partie blanche de la peau d'une orange'. Such words give you the opportunity to point out, as annoyingly as possible, how much richer the English language is compared with French. However, in the spirit of fair play (for which I am well known), I would like to mention 'une *version*' and 'un thème'. While we can only talk about doing a bit of translation for homework, the French have these two cunning words that tell you whether the work was from French or into French. Thus 'une *version*' is a translation exercise from a foreign language into French, while 'un thème' is a piece of work going the other way.

Vivement This sounds as though it ought to mean lively, which indeed it does. So, when a Truffaut film called *Vivement Dimanche* came out, I assumed it must be about a Sunday when particularly lively things happened. It was only later, when I heard someone say '*Vivement* le weekend', obviously looking forward to it, that I began to suspect another meaning. In fact *vivement* can also mean roll on or hurry up. In June you can hear people say, '*Vivement* les vacances', while, exhausted after a bad day at work, someone who can't wait for bedtime will sigh, '*Vivement* ce soir que l'on se couche.'

Voie This one is tricky because you are going to have to pronounce sounds in your head or out loud in order to follow my drift. We'll start with a comforting thought: the English are not the only ones to have trouble pronouncing French words. If you listen long enough, you will spot the fact that certain French people appear not to be able to pronounce parts of the verb 'voir' correctly. The word *voie* when it means a railway line or track poses no problem. Everyone happily says 'vwoah'. However, when faced with the subjunctive of the verb 'voir', which also includes forms such as 'voie', things go to pieces. Certain people – and we have already come across them – instead of saying 'vwoah' as they should, say 'vwoye'. This is particularly unattractive to the ear. You can try to reason with them, but it is usually to no avail. They believe that, because it is a verb, it should be pronounced 'vwoye'. It quite definitely shouldn't.

Vouvoyer We have seen that there is a handy French verb, TUTOYER, for addressing someone as 'tu'. There is an equivalent for calling someone 'vous' – *vouvoyer*. As you would expect, there is also a word corresponding to 'tutoiement', which, unsurprisingly, is 'vouvoiement'.

FRENCH FOREIGN WORDS

Bilingue I can feel myself getting annoyed already. This word irritates me enormously. *Bilingue* obviously means bilingual and should apply only to someone who is equally at ease in two languages. If you are not born into a bilingual family, it is going to take a good seven years' hard study to become more or less bilingual – if you are lucky. What I find intensely galling is the way the parents of French young people who spend a couple of weeks in the UK doing a summer job describe their offspring as *bilingue* once they return. How on earth they are daft enough to believe that two or three weeks working in a pizzeria in Basingstoke is going to make someone bilingual is beyond me. Try as you might, you will never convince these self-satisfied parents who say, 'Maintenant, il est bilingue' of their error, even if you speak English to their poor kids, whereupon it becomes perfectly clear that they can't understand a word you're saying. When I do this, they try to explain it away by saying that he or she isn't used to my accent.

And now that I am all uptight, I might as well mention the French people who do 'une licence d'anglais' – a degree in English – and think that this makes them internationally renowned linguists. Reading English is a soft option at a French university and doesn't actually require much knowledge of English. When someone says smugly, 'J'ai une licence d'anglais,' I tend to counter with, 'Don't worry, there's no need to apologize.' They look at me as though I am mad.

Bye-bye It is surprising how rarely you hear a French person say 'au revoir' as O Level French taught us they should when saying goodbye. The height of cool is to show off how many foreign words you know for taking your leave. One of the most common, especially among women, is '*bye-bye*', unfortunately in a silly French accent. This can be combined with something in French, ending up, for example, with 'Allez, *bye-bye*' or '*Bye-bye*, bon weekend', which is half of one and half of the other. Those with an affinity for things German, or perhaps Alsatian, will say 'Tchüss', doing their best to sound German, while admirers of Italian sign off with 'ciao'. I have a colleague who gets somewhat carried away and says 'Ciao, *bye-bye*' when she leaves every evening. Some jokers, inspired by the Italian farewell 'arrivederci', think it is most amusing to say 'arrivée d'air chaud'. As this means 'hot-air inlet', it isn't that amusing at all.

Début Can I ask you, when you use this word in English, to say, for example, 'Jack Smith made his debut as a singer back in 1981,' to pronounce it 'déb*u*' with a short, tight u, and not 'daybooo' as is so often heard on the BBC? Thank you.

Franglais I don't really know what else to call these words. There are quite a few words used in French that seem to be English words, but are in fact slightly odd. The most common is 'parking', which is French for car park. The French are convinced that it is the correct English term and will happily use it when speaking English, for example when asking of a friendly Londoner, 'Can you show me the way to the parking?' There are several fake words in the field of sports, notably 'un tennis man' for a male tennis player, and 'un record man' for a world-record holder. People who go running for pleasure refer to this activity as 'faire un footing'. However, this is ambiguous because others use the same term to mean going for a brisk walk. Try as you like, you won't convince anyone that these are not the proper English words for the things in question.

There are also odd plurals, for example where a plurality of English police officers is referred to as 'des policemans'. My favourite one of all was used by my dear sister-in-law who was considering adopting 'un boat people'.

Morceau de sucre We have seen when dealing with those who claim to be BILINGUE that the French often overestimate their abilities in English. Being only human, I often feel the urge to bring such people down a peg or two. A good question to ask, should you seek to do likewise, is how to say 'un *morceau de sucre*' in English. Ninety-nine times out of a hundred you will be rewarded by a smug smile and the answer 'a piece of sugar', sugar being pronounced with a very long a. 'Eh, non!' you can then say, 'Pas du tout – it is sugar lump,' before leaning back contentedly and enjoying their confusion.

VO/VF When a French cinema is showing a foreign film, the programme and the sign outside the cinema will specify either *VO* or *VF*. These stand for, respectively, 'Version Originale' and 'Version Française'. 'Version Originale' means that the film will be shown in its original language with French subtitles, while 'Version Française' means that it will be dubbed into French. Obviously, wherever possible, we go to see films 'en *VO*'. The only problem is that you can't help reading the subtitles to check whether they have translated things properly and occasionally you find that you have got behind with the plot. Seeing the film 'en *VF*' is worse though, as you catch yourself trying to lip-read what was actually said in the original. I have to confess I can only do this for the rude words.

Historical Matters and
Perfidious Albion

You will be relieved to discover that there is only one date that you really need to know in all of French history. You will also be treated to a sometimes painful look at how the English are seen by the French. Scots readers, on the other hand, will have a much easier time of it.

Other topics include an insight into what 'The Marseillaise' is truly about and the revelation of who it was who became famous just for saying 'Non!'

ENGLAND AND THE ENGLISH

Anglais The adjective used to describe an inhabitant of any country of the UK. French Anglophobes – yes, there really are such people – apply it to any visitor from any English-speaking nation, or, in extreme cases, from any foreign country at all, except possibly Germany. For example, in a sporting event between England and France, problems can arise when the referee is Irish. Explaining to people that Ireland is a completely independent country, as different from England as Sweden is from France, falls on deaf ears, and will not stop virulent allegations of bias based on the fact that the referee is *anglais*, presumably because he was heard speaking English.

Angleterre The French appear to have problems naming the extensive landmass and its neighbouring islands that lie between Calais and Iceland. We know this territory to be called the United Kingdom of Great Britain and Northern Ireland. The French think it is called 'l'*Angleterre*'. While they are aware that countries such as Scotland and Wales exist – indeed they use these terms quite correctly in the months of January, February and March during the Six Nations championship – they inexplicably refer to these countries at all other times as 'l'*Angleterre*'. A list of fruitless things to attempt in France must include trying to get a French person to understand the difference between 'la Grande Bretagne' and 'le Royaume Uni'. It's even harder than trying to explain the rules of cricket.

L'ennemi héréditaire (the traditional enemy) That is, the English.

'Messieurs les Anglais, tirez les premiers!' This is one of those quotes about the English that the French know but is almost unknown in England. My more erudite colleagues say it to me quite often. Apparently, at the start of the battle of Fontenoy in 1745, one of the major battles of the war of Austrian Succession, lengthy civilities including much raising of hats were exchanged between the English and French commanders. After finally replacing his hat, the French commander, Charles Hay, the Comte d'Auteroche, is reputed to have cried out this invitation to the English troops to shoot first. The strategic advantage of such an invitation is unclear in that a thousand French troops fell at the first English volley.

Perfide Albion It came as a considerable shock to discover, in the course of the first months I spent in France, that the country of my birth is not called 'l'ANGLETERRE' as I had for so long assumed. In conversation my colleagues referred to it exclusively as 'la *perfide Albion*' or perfidious Albion. Obviously, they weren't using it as a straightforward synonym for 'l'ANGLETERRE' because the expression implies a fair degree of criticism. Whenever I tried to argue that the English weren't that perfidious, my colleagues came up with numerous, incontrovertible examples of historical events which clearly showed that we are. The inhabitants of 'la *Perfide Albion*' remain, however, 'les Anglais' and not, as might be assumed, 'les perfides Albionnais' or some such.

Royaume Uni Unknown country, occasionally confused with l'ANGLETERRE.

PREFERRED NATIONS

Auld Alliance While the English are L'ENNEMI HÉRÉDITAIRE or 'la PERFIDE ALBION', the Scots are viewed in a far more favourable light. This is a result of a long-standing friendship between the countries which started in the thirteenth century. Both Scotland and France were having trouble with a belligerent England so it seemed wise that they join forces against a common foe. This pact was formalized in October 1295 and is known as the *Auld Alliance*. Its effects carried on well into the sixteenth century. Nowadays, you hear it mentioned only during the Six Nations championship, when both countries try their best to beat England. When I encounter a French Anglophobe, I take full advantage of the fact that my dad came from Scotland and claim to be Scots rather than English. It works a treat!

Les Belges Continuing the European theme, *les Belges* are the Belgians, a people who enjoy a particular reputation with the French which it would be uncharitable of me to discuss here. The reason I mention things Belgian is that several French icons are in fact Belgian. For a start there is Hergé, the creator of Tintin. He was Belgian and, incidentally, created his 'nom de plume' by taking his initials, G R, and turning them round to make R G, which, when pronounced in a French accent, gives Hergé. Not a lot of people know that! Then there is the renowned rock star Johnny Hallyday, who not only has Belgian roots but is, at the time of writing, actively trying to obtain Belgian nationality. The great comedian Raymond Devos was born in Belgium, as was the singer Jacques Brel. I'm sure most French people are absolutely convinced that all these are true Frenchmen.

HISTORICAL MATTERS

Ancien combattant While in no way am I going to discuss French success or failure in the various wars in which they have participated over the past thousand or so years, I do think that you should, nevertheless, know this. 'Un *ancien combattant*' is a war veteran or an ex-serviceman and it is a term that crops up more often than it does in the UK, where it is mainly heard on Remembrance Day. For a start, on public transport there are seats reserved for ex-servicemen. If someone wishes to claim one of these seats, he will have to brandish a card called 'une carte de priorité' in order to persuade whoever is occupying it to give up his seat. The few surviving veterans of the Great War are affectionately known as 'poilus' – hairy men – a reference to the difficulty they had shaving in the trenches. Those who were wounded in conflict are also entitled to priority seating and, more usefully, parking, but have to show a card or have a sticker on their car that proves them to be GIG or 'grand invalide de guerre'.

Jeanne d'Arc Nearly six hundred years on, she is still the subject of acrimony between the French and the British, or should I say between the French and me. The number of times that colleagues have reproached me with the words 'Vous avez brûlé *Jeanne d'Arc*' – the 'vous', I hope, meaning the English generally and not me personally – is considerable. Trying to argue that, given that it happened in 1431, it might no longer be a topical subject, falls on deaf ears. Similarly, seeking to pin the blame for the sorry affair on the Burgundians, rather than the English, won't do you any good either. You really can't forgive things like that. If you are accused of having, in some small way, participated in the burning of poor Joan, the only thing that seems to shut people up is to ask them to remind you when exactly it all took place. As they won't know but won't want to admit it, they will usually change the subject fairly rapidly. In case you are interested, it was 31 May 1431. If you want to know what she looked like, there is a splendid gold statue of Joan on horseback in Place des Pyramides opposite the Louvre, even though she was burned at the stake in Rouen. She has somehow ended up as the mascot for the French National Front party, which is possibly less glorious.

Marignan 1515

The only date that all English people are supposed to remember is that of the Battle of Hastings – 1066. Despite the fact that the Norman king William set off from Dives in Normandy, the French have never heard of 1066. The only date that everyone knows in France is *Marignan 1515* (pronounced 'quinze-cent-quinze'). What is generally less well known – I have conducted a survey on your behalf – is where Marignan actually is. Many think it is near Marseilles because they mix it up with Marignane, which is Marseilles airport. In fact Marignan is just outside Milan in Lombardy. The battle was fought, and won, by King François I, who led his army over the Alps to fight the Swiss, who were the allies of Pope Léon X. This was quite a feat because François had only just come to the throne, at the tender age of twenty-one. Having beaten the Swiss, the king had a chance encounter with Leonardo da Vinci and persuaded him to return with him to France, where Leonardo became involved in the design of Château de Chambord, which François was having built. This explains why Leonardo died in Amboise and not in his native Italy.

'La Marseillaise'

'God Save the Queen' is a charming and pleasant anthem calling on God to take care of the monarch. It has served Great Britain well for a considerable period of time. The French have 'La Marseillaise', a song written in 1792 by Claude-Joseph Rouget de Lisle, a captain of Engineers in the Rhine army. At that time, France had just declared war on Austria and Prussia and the army was preparing to go to Paris. The Mayor of Strasbourg approached de Lisle about composing a rousing tune for this march to the capital and de Lisle apparently did so that very night. The fact that the song was composed to inspire troops to defeat the enemy is obvious when you translate the words into English. A charming and pleasant anthem it is not. The first verse contains lines like:

> Do you hear in the countryside
> The roar of these savage soldiers?
> They come right into our arms
> To slaughter our sons and our wives.

Cheery stuff. But it gets worse when you reach the chorus. This ends with the following:

> March on,
> March on!
> May their impure blood
> Water our fields.

Just bear this in mind when you next watch on television a French team involved in an international match and hear 80,000 spectators lustily crying for blood.

Navarre This is a name only ever mentioned in the expression 'de France et de *Navarre*'. People declare that they have the best job, the finest house or whatever, in all of France and *Navarre*. Most of them have no idea where *Navarre* is or why it should so generously be included in French territory. In fact, it is actually a Spanish province that lies south of the Pyrenees and has the city of Pamplona as its capital. In 1589, Henri of *Navarre* became Henri IV of France as well and thus became the first of several sovereigns to be known as 'Roi de France et de *Navarre*'. The Kingdom was known as France and *Navarre* until *Navarre* was handed back to the Spanish.

Non! The most famous use of the French word *non* was by Charles de Gaulle – who is often called 'l'homme qui a dit "*Non!*"' While he said *non* to a variety of things – notably French Algeria and Britain's entry into the Common Market – his first and most famous *non* was in the speech known as 'l'appel du 18 juin' in 1940 after the French surrender. He said: 'Mais le dernier mot est-il dit? L'espérance doit-elle disparaître? La défaite est-elle définitive? *Non!*' – But has the last word been spoken? Must hope disappear? Is the defeat final? No! And, luckily for him, he was right!

Young People
(and Their Slang)

Young people need a section all to themselves. Having learned how to refer to kids of both sexes, we will see the sort of slang terms that they use. Of course, many of the words are also used by older people, even by parents.

You don't necessarily want to say these words in public – after all, you have your reputation to consider. I just want to improve your chances of recognizing what the teenagers standing behind you in the bus queue are going on about. Unfortunately, they might only be talking about bogs or cigarettes.

For those who have been waiting impatiently, there will at last be a couple of rude words.

YOUNG PEOPLE

Fille, meuf, nana The proper word for girl is *fille*. Young people, however, tend to say 'une *nana*' instead of 'une *fille*', and boys will say things such as, 'T'as vu la *nana* là-bas? Elle est trop belle!' or, when announcing a new girlfriend, 'Je viens avec ma nouvelle *nana*.' The craze for backslang, known as VERLAN, has produced a new word for girl based on the word for woman which is *femme*. Applying the turn it round backwards principle of backslang changes 'une femme' into 'une *meuf*'. So you'll hear young people talking about a party where there were 'beaucoup de jolies *meufs*'.

Dictionaries claim that girls can be referred to as 'souris' or mice, but I have never heard anyone say this.

Les filles!, Les garçons! The French have a whole range of ways of greeting several people at once which don't have an equivalent in English. A girl will greet a number of other girls collectively by saying, 'Salut *les filles!*' or urge them to hurry up and leave by yelling, 'Eh! *Les filles!* On y va?', whereas saying, 'Hello girls' or 'Come on girls' sounds as though you are at a ladies' hockey match in Cheltenham. Similarly, a group of boys can be hailed or greeted as *les garçons* or, more probably, 'les MECS' by a girl or a boy.

You can even refer to a group of your friends as 'les copains'. Imagine walking into a pub and saying, 'Hello friends'!

Mec, gars, type By far the most common word for a bloke is *mec*. The late lamented comedian Coluche started most of his jokes with the words 'C'est l'histoire d'un *mec* qui . . .' A particularly virile chap who deserves the respect of his peers will be referred to as 'un vrai *mec*'.

Alternative words for bloke are *gars* and *type*.

SLANG AND OTHER USEFUL WORDS

À poil A handy term with two principal meanings. While 'un poil' means a (body) hair, *à poil* doesn't mean hairy, as one might assume; it means stark naked. You can be caught *à poil* or spend a week in a naturist colony 'complètement *à poil*'. You can also build handy compound expressions such as 'se mettre *à poil*', which means to take off all your clothes. Apart from the stark naked meaning of the expression, you can also shout it out, for example to your friends, generally when you are outside and in a state of inebriation. Alternatively, you can shout it out in a theatre or nightclub when you want to insult the performer. In either case, *à poil*, when yelled raucously, means get off or get 'em off, depending on the circumstances.

It is important not to confuse *à poil* with 'au poil', which means just right or exactly. Even less should you confuse it with 'à la poêle', which sounds very similar but means pan-fried.

BD Walk round any French bookshop – known as 'une librairie' despite the fact that this might make you think of a library – and you will spot a huge range of cartoon books in quantities far greater than you would ever see in the UK. Cartoon books are known as 'bandes dessinées' but this is almost always shortened to *BD*. Practically all young people and many adults are addicted to *BD*, and I don't just mean the Astérix series or the Lucky Luke books; there are dozens of titles to choose from. As well as *BD* for children, there is a range for adults, some of which can be amazingly violent or almost pornographic. Take a trip to la FNAC and you will be astonished by the size of the *BD* section and by the number of people happily browsing there. La FNAC occasionally has book signings by popular *BD* authors and on such days the shop is absolutely packed.

Bordel An excellent word with all sorts of handy meanings. In its literal sense, 'un *bordel*' is a brothel and is obviously connected with the word bordello. However, the word also means a complete mess or a cock-up. When faced with a teenager's disgusting bedroom you could cry, 'Quel *bordel*!' or, if you are convinced that some plan is going to go badly wrong, you could predict the disaster with the words 'Ça va être le *bordel*!' Similarly, a long time spent stuck in a horrendous traffic jam could be described as 'C'était vraiment le *bordel*.' You can also use '*Bordel!*' as an exclamation or to lend extra weight to an order. Faced with a group of shouting angry people, you could attempt to calm things down by yelling, 'Arrêtez de crier, *bordel*!' The extra word makes your instruction longer and gives it more force. It won't necessarily work any better, though.

Chiottes It is time to descend to things lavatorial. The correct word for lavatory is 'toilettes', a word that doesn't seem to have the social stigma of the English toilet. The dictionary definition is 'un lieu d'aisance' but this is never used in real life. As well as these, there are probably as many words for the lavatory in French as there are in English. Perhaps the most common, and certainly my favourite is 'les *chiottes*'. This is the equivalent of the bog (or the bogs, as it's plural) and is amusing because it is the feminine form of 'chiot', which means puppy. When my parents-in-law bred dogs, there was much hilarity when someone rang up looking for a bitch puppy and enquired, 'Vous avez des *chiottes*?' Another word is 'les cabinets', giving the expression 'aller aux cabinets', which is most often used by children. All these words, as you will have noticed, are plural. Going well down the social scale, you come to 'les waters', a term that clearly comes from WC. The letters WC are also used in France but tend to be pronounced 'vay say' and not 'double vay say' for reasons which I have never established. If you are trying to be genteel, you can opt for 'le petit coin' or little corner, which is a rare singular term. Finally, many families seem to have their own word for the loo. My first boss went 'aux wouah wouah', while others adopt a modified form of the word 'cabinets' and go 'aux cabes'. Sadly, none of these comes even close to my favourite English euphemism, which is 'I am going to turn my bike round'!

Chouette   There are two common French words for owl: one is 'hibou', which you probably learned at school, the other is *chouette*. Feel free to forget the word 'hibou' for the time being. I seemed to hear the word *chouette* a lot when I first came to France but couldn't see why people were going on about owls all the time. In fact, *chouette* in general usage has nothing whatsoever to do with owls. It means wonderful, lovely, brilliant, kind, neat and more. A pretty girl is *chouette*, as is a flash car or a nice house. If you want to make clear that something is really particularly special, you can combine the word with VACHEMENT and declare whatever it is to be VACHEMENT *chouette*. An extremely pleasant person who is not necessarily beautiful can also be affectionately referred to as *chouette*. Incidentally, there is a very old joke about why owls are lucky. The answer, you will be delighted to learn, is because the wife of 'un hibou' is *chouette*.

Clope

The slang word for a cigarette is 'une *clope*'. Among young people, it is almost universally used; no one at all says 'une cigarette'. You can often hear them asking one another for a cigarette with the words, 'S'il te plaît. T'as pas une *clope*?' and meeting with a high success rate. A light for the cigarette is 'du feu' as in 'T'as du feu?' As the exchange is between young people, the 'tu' form of the verb is used, even though the two are complete strangers. It is a lesser known fact that while 'une *clope*' means a whole cigarette, 'un *clope*' means a cigarette end. If you want the whole thing, therefore, be careful to use the feminine form.

Con

You have probably been thinking, 'What about the rude words, then?' Well, while I have no intention of teaching you many rude French words, there is one that is really indispensable. What's more, it probably has the widest range of meanings of any French obscenity and thus is the hardest to translate into English. Its only advantage is that it is one of the shortest to write. As an adjective, *con* is simply translated as bloody stupid, whereas when used as a noun it means something like stupid git. When someone does something both stupid and annoying, the only thing you can reasonably cry out in your exasperation is 'Quel *con*!' – what a prat! There are also a number of longer words derived from the word *con*, but I'll let you look them up yourselves as they are very rude indeed. My first boss had a favourite phrase which implied, but didn't actually use, this word. When moaning about something daft that someone else had done, he liked to say, 'On est très peu à ne pas l'être' – There are very few of us who aren't . . . *con*. I was grateful when he said this to me because I then assumed that I was included in those who weren't. On good days, I might even have included him!

Contrepèterie This is a doubly hard word to deal with. First, you have to understand its meaning; second, and far harder, you have to understand the point of it all. *Contrepèterie* is the French translation of spoonerism, the accidental transposition of the initial letters of two words in a phrase, something for which the Rev. Spooner became famous. For example, he is reputed to have said, 'He has just received a blushing crow' instead of a crushing blow. All spoonerisms are relatively innocent and are usually accidental. *Contrepèteries*, on the other hand, are defined as 'interversion des lettres ou des syllabes d'un ensemble de mots produisant un sens burlesque, souvent obscène'. They are far from innocent – in fact, usually very rude – and always done deliberately. We shall turn to Rabelais for an example. He wrote 'femme folle à la messe' – crazy woman at mass, which was intended to make people think of 'femme molle à la fesse' – woman of soft buttocks. (This was quite racy stuff in Rabelais's day.) My problem is that whenever I am faced with a *contrepèterie*, I think, 'Oh, so what?' I really can't see the point at all. They tend to appeal mainly to young men in a state of inebriation. If you don't plan on spending time with such people, I wouldn't bother much with *contrepèteries*.

Dodo Nothing whatever to do with extinct flightless birds. *Dodo* is a familiar, or child's, word for sleep. Efforts to encourage a toddler to go to bed are based around sentences like 'Allez! C'est l'heure d'aller au *dodo*' or 'On va faire un gros *dodo*' and generally meet with as much success as they would in the UK.

The word also figures in a common expression that sums up the life of a commuter. This is said to consist of 'Métro, boulot, *dodo*' and roughly translates as commute, work, sleep.

Flotte, flotter That there are lots of slang words for things in French is not surprising. What strikes me as odd is that there are slang words for ordinary, everyday things – for book ('bouquin'), car ('bagnole') and even the wind ('zef'). There is also a common slang word for water, which is 'la *flotte*'. In its formal sense, 'la *flotte*' means the fleet (as in a lot of warships together). There is also a verb, *flotter*, which means to float. The floating sense and the fleet sense appear to have led to the modern meaning of water. The word is surprisingly common. At mealtimes, you will be asked to 'passer la *flotte*', while thirsty people will throw themselves on 'un verre de *flotte*' and reformed alcoholics drink 'que de la *flotte*'. As well as meaning to float, *flotter* means to rain. You look out of the window to check whether 'Il est toujours en train de *flotter*', while if you get caught in the rain, you say, 'J'ai pris la *flotte*.'

Génial! An immensely handy word, *génial* can simply be described as a stronger French version of the word nice. Everyone uses it, but teenagers especially would be incapable of describing anything favourably without it. You can flatter people with it – 'Vous êtes *génial*!'; you can enthuse about something – 'C'est *génial*!'; or just exclaim happily when faced with something special – '*Génial!*' For the opposite of *génial*, please see NUL. Both *génial* and NUL have other, proper meanings that are given in the dictionary.

Merde! I have said earlier that you won't find many rude words here. This one is included, not in its usual sense – the one you more than probably know – but because of a more friendly way in which it can be used. As well as being a multi-purpose insult that you yell at people when displeased with them, *merde!* can be used to wish someone luck. It is often thought unlucky to wish someone well for an exam or when they are about to go on stage in a play by saying 'Bonne chance!' It has become fairly common to say *merde!* instead, a bit like saying to an actor, 'Break a leg.' Thus, as you say goodbye before whoever it is sets off for their ordeal, you can add, 'Je te dis *merde!*' If you are a bit squeamish about actually coming out with the word in polite society, you can just leave it out and use a meaningful pause instead, saying, 'Pour demain, je te dis . . .' while nodding. Using *merde!* in this way is quite common: I have just heard a journalist on the radio say to the manager of the French rugby team 'Et . . . *merde!* pour samedi.'

Mince! As well as having a fairly comprehensive range of real, serious swear words, the French have a selection of nice, or mock swear words, which start with the same letter as the ruder word they are intended to replace. Thus, instead of the favourite French expletive MERDE! many people will say *mince!*, which not only starts with the same letter but also has the same number of letters. *Mince* means thin, which doesn't seem to make it that suitable for a swear word. The major problem is that in saying *mince* in an attempt to sound genteel, in many people's eyes you end up looking ridiculous.

Nul As we have seen with GÉNIAL, that all-purpose word for expressing enthusiasm and favour, the opposite is *nul*. While GÉNIAL is invariably pronounced in an enthusiastic manner with a rising intonation, *nul* is always muttered in a low, glowering tone. As with GÉNIAL, it is more the preserve of teenagers, especially grumpy ones grumbling about some minor irritant. 'C'est *nul*!' in an aggrieved voice marks the depths of displeasure. The more upset the teenager, the longer the 'u' in the middle of the word. While you are hardly likely to exclaim 'Wouah! C'est *nuuul*' when visiting a BOULANGERIE on holiday, even if they have sold out of your favourite cakes, you could always while away some time by sidling up to a group of adolescents and counting the number of mentions of GÉNIAL and *nul*.

Oh la la! Everyone knows that French people say *oh la la!* when surprised in some way, and I am certainly not going to tell you that they don't. What is interesting is that not all French people seem to say exactly the same thing. Years of attentive listening have convinced me that variations are possible and even commonplace. Everyone uses the same syllables, of course. It is just the number of syllables, particularly the 'las', that varies. Friends and colleagues regularly put in an extra 'la', whether for emphasis or because they can't manage to stop in time. However, the resulting three 'las' appear to be considered insufficient, or possibly asymmetric, because it is more common to hear four 'las' rather than three. In either case, the final 'la' is noticeably stronger than the preceding ones. This extra stress on the last one seems to increase the more 'las' there are. With the basic *Oh la la* the two 'las' are practically indistinguishable, whereas with *Oh la la la la!* the last 'la' is not only stressed but drawn out much longer than the other three. I have a colleague who is the only person I know who, in moments of extreme emotion, will exclaim *Oh la la la la la* la*!*, the last 'la' lasting as long as all the others put together.

Ouais Any young English-speaking person generally says yeah instead of yes. Apart from probably not wanting to conform, they most likely do it because yeah is easier to pronounce and requires less muscle effort than that needed to say yes brightly. Not wishing to be outdone by their British counterparts, French-speaking youth tends to say *ouais* instead of 'oui' for pretty much the same reasons. To say *ouais*, like saying yeah, just involves letting your mouth fall open, while making a sound pretty much like grunting. Saying 'oui', on the other hand, makes you draw the sides of your mouth apart in a tiring rictus. Also, people in general tend to show scepticism at an idea by replying 'Mmmouais'. This starts off with a sort of humming through closed lips, followed by an elided *ouais*.

In the Lucky Luke cowboy cartoon books, in order to imitate real cowboys who say yep!, Lucky Luke says 'ouap'.

Pote We will see that COPAIN is a slang word for friend. Another one, *pote*, while it also means friend, implies that it is a particularly good friend, one of the best. By saying of someone 'C'est un *pote*,' you make it clear that it is someone whom you appreciate and can rely on. If you want to show that he is extra special, you will refer to him as 'C'est un bon *pote*.' A bloke walking into a bar to find his mates already there will greet them collectively with the words 'Salut les *potes*!' This notion of special friendship led to the word being adopted in a campaign against racism where support for immigrants was based on the slogan 'Touche pas à mon *pote*!' – Hands off my mate! – set out on a badge shaped like the palm of a hand.

Punaise/purée As we have seen, people use the word MINCE! as a substitute for the common or garden MERDE! The list of French swear words also includes the far stronger, and much less pleasant word (which you should on no account use), 'putain'. If applied to someone, this means whore or slut, but it can also be used as a sign of exasperation or anger, when it more commonly becomes 'Oh! Putain!' However, as this is quite strong, there are a couple of words that sound vaguely similar and can be used instead, in much the same way as some people exclaim 'Oh! Sugar!' instead of 'Oh! Shit!' These are *punaise*, which literally means drawing pin or a variety of beetle, and *purée*, which means mashed potato. Clearly, anyone shouting 'Drawing pin!' or, worse, 'Mashed potato!' at moments of extreme emotion is someone to be treated with suspicion.

Quoi . . . ? In the UK, young people shower their sentences with filler words such as like and I mean, not to mention you know. In France, the single word without which young people would go into spasm each time they tried to say anything is *quoi*. This means what but is generally tacked on to the end of a more or less coherent sentence to show that they have got to the end of it, such as it is, and that it's probably your go now. A variant on the theme is to finish with the words 'voilà, *quoi*'. This means: 'That's all that I have to say on the matter so there is no point in hoping for any more.' The word 'voilà' is spoken with a rising intonation, while the *quoi* finishes on a falling one. Schoolteachers love to ask their pupils to make a brief presentation to the class without ending it with 'bien, voilà, *quoi*.' Very few of them manage it.

Rigoler How many words are there in English for laughing? If you think for a while, you will realize that there aren't that many synonyms for laughter or laugh. You can check, if you like, in a thesaurus. There are words such as chuckle, chortle, giggle or snigger, but these are low-key affairs and don't really imply loud, memorable laughter. Of course, there are expressions such as rolling on the floor laughing or splitting my sides with laughter, but there aren't any words which by themselves mean laughing out loud and enjoying the experience. It must be an indication of some aspect of the French character that they have lots of laughter words. The basic word for to laugh is 'rire', which you probably knew. But there are others, some colloquial, for laughing out loud such as 'se marrer', 's'esclaffer', 'se bidonner', *rigoler*, 'pouffer' or 'se poiler'. All these convey a notion of loud, joyous, hearty laughter that English words don't seem to manage. Once you have learned them all, you will realize that French people tend to have their own favourite, which they use all the time.

Sympa One of the first English words that foreign students learn is nice. As soon as they have, they can make up a whole range of simple sentences in which they describe things that they like as nice and things that they don't like as not nice. You will be pleased to learn that there is a French word that can be used as widely as nice to describe things that you like. The word is 'sympathique' but it is commonly abbreviated to *sympa*. Of someone you like, or who has been kind to you, you would say, 'Il est *sympa*' or even 'Il est très *sympa*.' If someone does something nice, you could thank them not with a simple 'merci' or even 'merci beaucoup' but by saying, 'Merci, c'est *sympa*.' It can also be used ironically when someone makes you do something that you didn't want to: 'C'est *sympa*!'

As with not nice, you can define many things, people or even places, as being 'pas *sympa*' or 'pas très *sympa*'. An unfriendly person would be described as 'Il n'est pas très *sympa*' or, if he was really unpleasant, 'Il n'est pas *sympa* du tout.' Once you have started using *sympa*, you will wonder how you ever managed without it.

Ta gueule! This is almost indispensable, either if you want a quiet life, or if you are planning on having a row with someone, for it means shut up. 'Gueule' is literally the muzzle of an animal, but it has come to mean a person's face. If you don't like the look of someone, you would say that 'Il a une sale gueule' or 'Je n'aime pas sa gueule.' *Ta gueule!* is used exactly like shut up so I don't need to give you any examples. Please note, though, that the fact that the expression is constructed in the 'tu' form does not mean that, should you find yourself having a violent argument with a stranger, or your boss, you should try to construct it in the 'vous' form. Saying 'votre gueule!' to an unpleasant stranger is unimaginably absurd. In any case, if you have reached the point where you are forced to say *Ta gueule!* to a stranger, you are past worrying about his sensibilities. There are, however, those who, when faced with several noisy individuals, typically children, tend to shout 'Vos gueules!' to them all rather than *Ta gueule!* individually.

A politer way of asking someone to stop talking is to say 'Tais-toi' or 'Taisez-vous', as the need arises.

Truc In English we have a thingy or a whatsit or the like to define an object that we can't be bothered to name correctly or don't actually know the name of. In French you must learn two vital words as soon as possible to have any chance of understanding what people are talking about. They are *truc* and 'machin', both of which mean thing. Asking for something in a shop when you don't know what it is called becomes so much easier when you can say that you are looking for 'Un *truc* qui fait . . .' going on to explain what it does, possibly waving your hands about to help make yourself understood. *Truc* can also be used for the solution to a problem or a cunning way of dealing with something. You would boast about this by saying 'J'ai trouvé le *truc*!' The word 'machin' can be used even for a person you don't know, or can't be bothered to name, though this is exceedingly uncomplimentary. There are compound words that mean the same thing as *truc* but are more entertaining, such as 'machin-chouette' or even 'un machin-*truc*' when you really have *no idea* what else to call it.

Vachement Reading this you probably thought that it has something to do with cows. Think again. *Vachement* means amazingly or extremely and is the slang word that is used in place of proper words such as 'extrêmement' or 'particulièrement'. The majority of young people – and quite a few others – would be hard put to have a conversation without using it. Whether you are describing how pretty the girl was – 'Elle était *vachement* jolie' – or how fast the bloke on the motorbike was going – 'Il allait *vachement* vite' – or how expensive it was – 'C'était *vachement* cher' – you really can't do without it. Despite appearances, though, it has nothing to do with cows whatsoever.

Verlan This is the French form of backslang – a way of creating new slang words by reversing the order of the syllables of an existing word. The translation of backwards is 'à l'envers'. If you take 'à l'envers' and apply the principle of backslang to it, you end up with *verlan*. *Verlan* is most common among the young people in the poorer suburbs of Paris, but is so widespread that practically all young people use a word now and again, sometimes unknowingly. A common example is MEUF instead of 'femme' as we have seen under FILLE, but all sorts of common words have their *verlan* equivalent, to the bemusement of many parents. When upset or uptight, people used to be 'énervé'; now, they are 'vénère'. You no longer call your mother 'ma mère' but 'ma rem', and you describe tedious people not as 'lourd' but as 'relou'. I even know of someone whose dog – 'le chien' – is referred to as 'le ienche'.

Relations (Family and Others)

It is sad to think that you have probably been walking into French shops in silence. All that is soon to change! This section deals with meeting and greeting people and includes a few words to do with people whom you know rather better than others. A beginner's guide to kissing on the cheeks is followed by the real reason why certain professionals attach plastic bags to trees.

You will also find a selection of words relating to members of the family, from very young to quite old.

GREETINGS AND EXPRESSIONS

Au plaisir! There is an expression, '*Au plaisir* de vous revoir', which the dictionary defines as being a friendly salutation when taking your leave. It roughly translates as looking forward to seeing you again and can be used, for example, when saying goodbye politely to someone whom you have just met. Alternatively, a salesperson, or someone who has been providing some kind of service to a customer, may use it after saying goodbye. However, the whole expression is rarely used. You are much more likely to hear someone say just '*au plaisir!*', as an alternative to 'au revoir'. There is a slight problem, though, because, to put it bluntly, saying *au plaisir!* is thought a bit vulgar by certain people. My esteemed family-in-law has trained me to believe that several words in these pages are considered common, and that this expression is among the worst. Rather than take their word, perhaps you should listen out for this and other expressions and judge for yourself.

BCBG Four letters which sum up an entire lifestyle. They stand for 'bon chic, bon genre', which roughly means someone who dresses tastefully and comes from a good family. Calling a person *BCBG* conveys the fact that they not only look nice but may be assumed to buy quality, fashionable clothes which will suit them. If that wasn't enough, such people, given that they come from a good family, can confidently be expected to behave well. If someone says, 'Elle est très *BCBG*,' everyone knows what to expect. A style of clothes could be described as 'un look *BCBG*'.

The late comedian Jacques Villeret declared that the letters in fact stood for 'beau cul, belle gueule', which means 'nice bum, nice face'.

Bon appétit! This is an expression used by practically everyone in France with the notable exception of my family-in-law, who resolutely maintain that it is common. Of course, if someone says it to you at the start of a meal, it is only polite to say it back. The problem is that you often get asked by French people how to say *Bon appétit!* in English. Things start to go downhill then because you are forced to admit that there is no real equivalent and that they should resort to something long-winded like 'I hope you enjoy your meal.' There is always the risk of someone unkindly pointing out that of course there is no need for such an expression in the UK because British food is so bad that no one can be expected to enjoy a meal there. It is wise at this point to distract whoever it is by getting the conversation off food and on to sex as quickly as possible, if circumstances permit, to avoid things degenerating rapidly.

Bonne continuation I can translate all the words in this book into English except this one. I know what it means and when it is used, but have really no idea of its English equivalent. *Bonne continuation* is like 'bon courage' in that it is a throw-away, friendly sort of thing that you say to someone at the end of a conversation, however brief. Waiters, for example, say it when they have brought a new dish to the table. Also, people who have been talking to you while you are doing something, and who leave you to get on with it, say it as they go away. It means something like I hope that you carry on enjoying whatever it is that you are currently doing, and preferably enjoying it even more than you did before we started talking. In the case of a meal, the waiter wants you to carry on enjoying your food and having a good time. In the case of some other activity, it means a cross between carry on, keep up the good work and have a nice day. I really can't be more specific than that.

Bon . . ., Bonne . . .
Following on from the previous entry, you can create a friendly expression to suit pretty much any occasion simply by starting it with *bon* or *bonne*. You can wish someone a nice day with '*Bonne* journée', a safe journey by saying '*Bonne* route', or '*Bon* retour' for a good trip back. And there is no real limit to this: someone announcing that they are going to put their washing on can be encouraged with a friendly '*Bonne* lessive', or you can even show support for someone's tidying up by saying '*Bon* rangement' without sounding in the least silly.

Bonjour, m'ssieurs, dames
Just listen next time you go into any bar or small shop in France, and you will hear people using the all-purpose, universal salutation *Bonjour, m'ssieurs, dames* as they walk in. Practically everybody says it. It is an abbreviated form of 'Bonjour, messieurs, mesdames' – which should, in fact, more correctly be 'Bonjour, mesdames, bonjour, messieurs' – a complete and formal greeting that is almost never used. Translated into English it sounds like a compère walking on to a stage and greeting the audience by saying, 'Good morning, ladies and gentlemen'; in French it passes for a collective hello. The only essential thing is that there must be two or more people present when you open the door and walk in. The 'bonjour' part can even be dropped leaving the shortened greeting 'Messieurs, dames', which can be further pared away to leave just 'M'sieurs, dames'. The reply to this universal salutation is, however, different. You cannot reply to a *Bonjour, m'ssieurs, dames* with your own *Bonjour, m'ssieurs, dames*;

it just doesn't work. It would be illogical and sound daft because you would not be greeting several people at once, but only the latest person to walk into the shop or bar you're in. You should therefore limit your reply to a simple 'Bonjour' or, if you are feeling formal, the more specific 'Bonjour, monsieur' or 'Bonjour, madame'.

Pardon? In English, if you haven't heard what someone has said and want them to repeat it, you can choose between several words, including Sorry?, What?, Pardon? or simply Eh? The French have a similar choice. Probably the most formal is *Pardon?*, which, if you want to go over the top, can be extended to '*Pardon?* Pouvez-vous répéter?' Or even, if you really want to make an issue of it, you can say, 'Je vous demande *pardon.*' But, of course, in real life, no one says that. What they do say most often is 'Comment?', the tone and the accent varying to suit the situation. Further down the scale comes 'Quoi?', which roughly corresponds to the English What?, and then, near the bottom of the scale, is a sound, rather than a word, which is spelled 'Hein?' This can only be pronounced properly if you curl your upper lip and wrinkle your nose. This is the French version of Eh? Finally, you can still occasionally encounter charming elderly people of the old school who, instead of saying the formal *Pardon?*, use the very polite and extremely old-fashioned, 'Plaît-il?' If you want to stand out from the crowd next time you are in France, try saying 'Plaît-il?' instead of *Pardon?*

Re- If you have ever felt that a French person has growled at you for no apparent reason, this may provide the explanation. When you meet someone for the first time on a given day, whether it is in the office or outside, you of course say 'Bonjour'. But what if you bump into them again in the course of the same day? Typically what happens is that one person will say 'Bonjour' again, then remember that you have already seen each other that day and correct the greeting to '*Re*-bonjour', where the *Re*- means again. This is all very well and good. But there are those who, instead of saying '*Re*-bonjour', drop the key part of the greeting and just say *Re*-. This sounds like a growly sort of 'Rruh!' Thus, through no fault of your own, you can find yourself growled at, though at least now you know why.

Salut! The Italian greeting 'Ciao' has always struck me as incredibly handy because you can use it both when you meet someone and when you take your leave from them. To the best of my knowledge, there is no comparable hello/goodbye word in English. The French, however, can claim one up on the Brits because they have got one of their own. It is *Salut!* It is far less formal than 'Bonjour' and is commonly used between friends who don't need to stand on ceremony. A brief survey in my office revealed that six out of seven colleagues greeted me by saying *Salut!* Most young people would be hard put to greet their contemporaries without using it. You can combine *salut* with other words to give greetings such as '*Salut* les MECS!' or '*Salut* les COPAINS!'

Incidentally, the French equivalent of the Salvation Army is 'l'Armée du Salut'. This does not mean the greetings army as *Salut* in this context means salvation.

SEX, OR AS CLOSE AS WE ARE GOING TO COME TO IT

Baiser We are going to have a minor blip in the alphabetical order as I need to explain this word before the next one. If you thought that this is the French for to kiss, think again. I am sure that I am not the only one to have been taught at school that this was what it meant, happily writing something like 'Le monsieur baise sa femme' in my O Level exam. Unfortunately, as a verb, *baiser* in fact means to screw, or whatever vulgar term you prefer for the act of procreation, and involves a far greater degree of intimacy than mere kissing. I wonder if whoever corrected my O Level script knew this. Perhaps it explains my B grade? The proper, current word for to kiss is 'embrasser'. However, when used as a noun 'un *baiser*' does indeed mean a kiss, girls asking their boyfriends 'Donne-moi un *baiser*' without any intention of this leading to any unseemly activity. Slightly lower down the intimacy scale comes 'un bisou', which means something along the lines of a peck on the cheek. You can also use terms like 'bons baisers' or 'gros bisous' to finish a letter where, in English, you would put love and kisses.

Baise-en-ville Having learned about the verb BAISER, you are now in a position to appreciate this. A *baise-en-ville* literally means having it off in town and refers to a small bag intended to carry the essential necessities required for an illicit rendezvous. Such a tryst usually, or so I am told, takes place in the early evening and thus is known as 'un cinq à sept'. I once had a colleague who carried one of those small leather bags with a strap, about the size of a book, which were all the rage in France a few years ago. He resolutely referred to this bag as his *baise-en-ville* even though it contained nothing more exotic than his keys, cigarettes and a pack of Kleenex.

Bise 'La *bise*' is the act of kissing someone on both cheeks. Mastering it is more difficult than it looks. As in kissing someone's hand (where you don't actually kiss it), kissing someone involves putting your cheek to the other person's and making a kissing sound rather than actually smacking your lips into their cheek. Clearly, two people can't kiss each other's cheeks at the same time as the angles don't work. Practice it in the privacy of your own home before letting yourself loose on your first victim, bearing in mind that it is vitally important to keep your lips away from theirs. Once you have mastered the act of kissing, you have to decide what sort of kisser you are going to be. There are people who kiss twice, some who kiss three times, others who kiss four times. There are also self-appointed experts who will talk at length on what sort of person will kiss a given number of times, and there are even those who try to draw parallels between particular regions of France and the number of kisses given. Such people will quote particular villages deep in rural France (of which there are an awful lot) where all the inhabitants give a single *bise*. Experience has taught me to be extremely sceptical of all this. As far as I can see, you can never tell what sort of kisser you may be confronted with.

If you decide that you are a two-kiss person, everything is fine as long as you are faced with fellow two-kiss people. However, if you encounter a four-kiss person, for example at a friend's house, things tend to go to pieces. You will do your two kisses to your fellow guest and then start to pull away, believing that the job is done. They, on the other hand, will only be half-way through their planned four-kiss routine and will be leaning forward for the third one. Noting to your horror that they haven't pulled away but are going for a third kiss, you will rapidly lean back to accept it. Either you will bump noses at this point, or the other person, having by then realized that you were going to do only two kisses, has started to pull away too, cutting matters short. In that case, you may well end up chasing them backwards, trying desperately to finish the four kisses that you have now belatedly set about. When a group of people with different kissing habits meet or say goodbye you may hear someone doing four kisses and note the fact. Unfortunately, they may have heard you doing your two kisses and therefore decided to do only two to you when your turn comes. Thus the four-kiss person will be about to do two kisses, while you, trying to fit in with them, will be about to change and do four. Chaos generally ensues. Some people, obviously more aware of the problem than others, resort to announcing the number of *bises* in advance, saying things like 'Moi, c'est quatre.' It has been suggested that some kind of sign or hand signal should be adopted in order to show in advance what kind of kisser you are. This strikes me as an excellent idea but I am not sure who to approach to try to get it set up. L'Académie Française perhaps?

Finally, there are even differences in the sounds people make during 'la *bise*', ranging from near silence to extraordinarily loud smacking sounds made from the opposite corner of their mouth to the other person's cheek.

Câlin When a small child is upset, or in need of comfort or reassurance, he or she will generally go to a parent or close friend and ask, 'Tu me fais un *câlin*?' 'Un *câlin*' is a hug or a cuddle. Similarly, when people show kittens, puppies or other little furry animals to a small child, they will urge the child to stroke it by saying, 'Tu lui fais des *câlins*?' The term can also be used as an adjective. For example, a parent will be heard saying of their off-spring, 'Il est très *câlin*,' when they mean that the child is a bit delicate and likes to be hugged and made a fuss of occasionally. (And who among us doesn't?) There are, yet again, those who say that *câlin* is used only by people in the lower social orders. The term can also refer to something of a far more sexual nature, the sort of thing that generally occurs only between consenting adults. I discovered this when a large female colleague explained her late arrival at work one morning by the fact that her husband 'a voulu faire un gros *câlin*' before leaving for the office. My colleagues and I were appalled and unanimously felt that this was too much information.

Copain, copine

When I first spent time in France I was lucky enough to do so in the company of a delightful young lady who, when I referred to her in English, I was proud to call my girlfriend. But how should I refer to her in French? It seemed, at the time, that I had the choice between the somewhat old-fashioned 'ma petite amie' and the more modern 'ma *copine*'. 'Ma petite amie', when pronounced in my charming English accent, invariably made people smile so I thought I'd go for 'ma *copine*'. In general, 'une *copine*' is the slang term for a female friend, a male friend being 'un *copain*'. Changing this to 'ma' or 'mon' alters the meaning from just a friend to girlfriend or boyfriend. Thus, introducing someone as '*un copain*' is quite different from saying 'Je vous présente *mon copain*.' There are girls who prefer to make things quite clear and refer to a friend as 'un *copain*', while their boyfriend is known as 'mon petit *copain*' – even if he is quite tall.

Later on, when you reach the age of live-in partners, *copain/copine* is no longer suitable, and people refer to such partners simply as 'mon ami' or 'mon amie', only the silent e indicating the sex.

Fête, boum, soirée, teuf

One of the principal signs of impending old age in France typically occurs shortly after your thirtieth birthday and centres on that terrible moment when you realize that you no longer know what to call a party. Party – a word I use for want of a better one to define a social evening where several adolescents or young people gather in the presence of loud music and alcohol – is tricky to translate into French. Each generation has had its own word for party. No sooner have you learned it than it is out of date. As far as I can see, those who are now grandparents called such a function 'une *soirée*' – or evening. Those who are parents used to go to 'une *boum*'. This is witnessed by a film from the early 1980s (starring the incomparable Sophie Marceau) called *La Boum*. Those who are younger attend 'une *fête*', while those who are younger still use the backslang (VERLAN) version of the word *fête*, which is *teuf*. Don't bother learning any of these – they are doubtless already out of date. If you want to ask a young person if they are going to a party, it is best to use a neutral expression like 'Est-ce que vous sortez ce soir?' and hope that you will recognize the word used in reply.

Marques d'affection

The British are remarkably restrained when it comes to terms of endearment – they call loved ones darling, sweetie, dear, honey, but nothing terribly surprising. The French, on the other hand, run the whole gamut from animal to vegetable. Unfortunately, I can't think of a mineral example. Most of the odder endearments, it must be said, are addressed to small children. Let's start with things animal: it is quite common to hear a mother address her toddler as 'ma puce' without anyone batting an eyelid. I have always found this odd as 'puce' means flea. Moving up the scale, kids can also be referred to as 'ma caille', which means quail, or sometimes 'ma poulette', or chicken. Am I the only one to find nothing endearing in either a flea or a quail – or even a chicken? As to things vegetable, many loving mothers call their small off-spring 'mon chou', which sounds quite sweet until you remember that 'chou' means cabbage. (OK, I admit that 'chou' is actually used in its alternative meaning of puff pastry in this context, but even that isn't very flattering.) Other common terms are 'mon canard' or my duck and 'mon sucre d'orge', which means my barley sugar.

Sac en plastique This, you won't be surprised to learn, is French for plastic bag. Some people abbreviate it to 'sac plastique', but it is probably better to stick to the whole thing. If you go south and find yourself beyond the Garonne river, you will have to learn to ask for 'une poche' instead of 'un *sac en plastique*', otherwise you won't get one. However, the real point of this paragraph is to explain what conclusion to draw if you find yourself driving through a forest in the Paris area and spot a plastic bag tied to a tree by the roadside. Assuming it has been tied, and not simply blown there, this indicates that there is a lady of the night waiting for customers in a clearing immediately by the tree with the bag. Should you desire to avail yourself of her services (or possibly of *his* services – although you won't necessarily be able to spot this at first glance), there is something else you need to know. If she is in a van, open curtains indicate that she is available for business; drawn curtains mean that she is currently engaged and you should return later. And to think that the last time you came across one, you thought it was just a bag tied to a tree!

FAMILY MEMBERS, YOUNG AND OLD

Arheu If you are going to have anything to do with babies in France, or speak to anyone who has one, this is a key word, or rather sound. For French babies do not gurgle and they certainly don't imitate their British cousins by going goo. French babies say *arheu, arheu*. So does anyone who talks to a baby. Unfortunately, this is a fiendishly difficult sound for English speakers who can't roll their Rs. Since it appears to be mandatory to say it when faced with a French baby, you have the choice between avoiding babies altogether, or trying to say it and sounding painfully English. Have a go anyway, and comfort yourself with the thought that the baby won't care how bad your accent is.

Le petit, la petite People have children in France. No surprises so far. What is different is the way they are referred to by members of their families. In Britain, parents with several kids may introduce them to visitors by saying, 'This is my eldest, George, and this is our youngest, Fiona.' In France, terms corresponding to the oldest and the youngest are also used, and may take on such importance that they end up replacing the children's actual names. The youngest child of three or more, and occasionally the younger of two, will be known as *le petit* or *la petite* according to sex, and this will go on at least until the child reaches twelve – and often beyond. Sometimes this leads to one parent asking the other, 'T'as vu *la petite*?' and not 'T'as vu Martine?' If the children are close in age or in size, it can be confusing for third parties who can't readily spot which one is *la petite*.

Where there are three or more children, the eldest may be known as 'la grande' or 'le grand'. The one in the middle is probably the only one to be called by their real name. It is not clear what parents write on labels for Christmas presents.

Pépé, Mémé, Papy, Mamie

You may have been troubled by the question of how the French refer to their grandparents. The correct individual words for 'les grandparents' are 'grandpère' and 'grandmère'. While these are the *correct* terms, there are other words that you should know, though not necessarily use. For, as with so many things, the choice of word is a function of certain social conditions. If you are from a titled family, or want to pretend that you are, you may refer to your elders as 'bonne-maman' and 'bon-papa'. If you descend below the level of 'grandpère et grandmère', you will know your parents' parents as '*Papy* et *Mamie*'. And why not? Calling them '*Pépé* et *Mémé*', on the other hand, starts to get worrying, while those who receive presents signed 'Pépère et Mémère' will be unlikely to be invited to our house. However, the word 'pépère', given that it conjures up images of portly, placid old men, can be used as an adjective meaning peaceful or easygoing, or to describe, for example, an untaxing job or a friendly old dog.

Pipi, caca

We have seen that the word ARHEU is vital if you come across French babies. But what happens if you have to talk to small French children? If you spend any length of time with them, it is likely at some point that the question of bodily functions will arise. But how should you refer to them? There are two principal words in common usage, one for each function: *pipi* and *caca*. A simple rule will suffice before we move on: *pipi* is OK, *cáca* quite definitely isn't.

Day-to-day Life

Here are some words that you will come across in newspapers, magazines or when watching the news. Mind you, my favourite is the one about suppositories, and you won't find them mentioned often on the news.

Buying a bed is harder than you thought, while tuning a musical instrument turns out to be a lot easier.

Arme blanche This is one of the French expressions whose meaning you can't fathom despite the fact that you understand the two words that make it up. *Arme blanche* means literally white weapon, but this is no help because the thing in question is not actually white at all, though it is indeed a weapon. 'Une *arme blanche*' is the commonly used term for a knife, more specifically a knife used for stabbing people in a fight rather than one used in a kitchen – even though these are often one and the same. You come across it in news reports when assorted thugs are described as fighting or attacking each other 'à l'*arme blanche*'. 'Blanche' apparently refers to the fact that a knife is made of steel, and thus could conceivably be viewed as white when opposed to the bronze used in other types of weapon, such as handguns.

Bic Each country seems to choose particular trade names to turn into common words for everyday objects. The British have opted for Hoover and Thermos, as well as taking the name of the original inventor of the ballpoint pen to describe the pen itself. Mr Biro has thus become immortalized, at least in the UK. Unfortunately, calling for 'un biro' in France will not result in anyone lending you their ballpoint pen. Instead you will have to ask, 'Pouvez-vous me prêter un *bic*, s'il vous plaît?', even though the pen that you will be lent will more likely have come from Japan than from Baron Bich's factories in France.

Since its success in producing simple ballpoint pens, the Bic company has branched out into making disposable lighters and even surfboards, though these products are not referred to as *bics*.

Bis An interesting little word that can be used in two different ways. The first place that you will most likely spot it is on house numbers. If a new house is built between number 24 and number 26, it will not be known as 24a, as it might in the UK, but will rejoice in the name of 24*bis*. *Bis* (pronounced beece, not biz) means doubling up, or doing again. If another house is put up between 24*bis* and number 26, it will be known as 24ter. *Bis* is also the word that you shout out at French concerts, whereas, ironically enough, were you in the UK, you would shout 'Encore'. It is meant to encourage the musician to repeat the piece he has just sung or played, rather than to encourage him to come back and perform something extra. From the musician's point of view, he has been 'bissé' by his enthusiastic audience.

Chiffres French numbers are tricky. The complex French counting system is explained under NUMÉROS DE TÉLÉPHONE later on. But, as well as counting difficulties, there are also complicated traps with numbers that don't take an s in their plural forms, when you could reasonably think that they should. While 'cinq cents' and 'cinq millions' each has an s at the end, the word for thousand – 'mille' – is INVARIABLE and thus doesn't take an s even when you write 'dix mille'. 'Cent' is, however, even trickier than 'mille' because while 'cinq cents' has an s, as soon as you add any words after the 'cents' it loses it. Thus, you write 'cinq cent trente' or 'six cent quarante-trois' without an s on the end of 'cent'. Finally, there is the question of numbers with hyphens. Strictly speaking, when you write the numbers between sixty and ninety-nine, you should scatter hyphens about the place. Thus, you should write 'soixante-dix' or 'quatre-vingt-douze' and not 'soixante dix 'or 'quatre vingt douze', even though practically no one does so any more. If, by any chance, you are still following all this, and haven't already moved on to the next word, 'vingt' in numbers like 'quatre-vingts' behaves like 'cent' in that it only takes a final s when there are no other words after it.

Coup de cœur You can't go into a record shop, a bookshop or a restaurant without having a fair chance of seeing this. In any review of books, records or wine, one of them will be selected as being someone's *coup de cœur* or particular favourite. A bookshelf containing the latest bestsellers will include a handwritten note by one of the members of the bookshop's staff setting out the reasons why a particular book has been especially enjoyed. This will be labelled as 'notre *coup de cœur*'. Similarly, in restaurants which put up a board with a chalked-up list of dishes of the day, they will also suggest the wine of the month, which is invariably called their *coup de cœur*. The use of this term rather than something neutral like 'le vin du mois' is intended to make you believe that someone really has tried it and liked it so much that they honestly feel your life will be improved by drinking it too. In fact, they are doing you a favour by mentioning it.

Dégriffé I had great difficulty understanding this word, mainly because I didn't know what 'griffé' was. I only knew the first sense of the word 'griffe', which is claw, 'griffé' thus meaning clawed. There is, however, another equally common meaning of 'une griffe', which is a designer label, mark or signature. This is what the perfume brand 'Ma griffe' is referring to and not, as I had originally supposed, someone's claw. Designer-label clothes are referred to as 'griffés'. When they are sold off at the end of a season in a discount saleroom, the designer labels are ripped out. The clothes are then '*dégriffés*' or unbranded, end-of-the-line reductions. You hear women showing off their new dress or coat, boasting about how cheaply they bought it as it was '*dégriffé*'.

18 (dix-huit) What do you do in the event of an emergency in France? In the UK, there is one phone number to dial whatever situation you find yourself in; in France, of course, things are different. If you want the police, it is simple: you dial 17. However, if you are faced with any kind of accident or life-threatening incident, then you call the fire brigade or 'les pompiers' by dialling *18*. 'Ah,' I hear you say, 'but what do I dial if I want an ambulance?' Simple: you call the fire brigade. If it is a real emergency – a fire, road traffic accident or whatever – you are expected to deal with the 'pompiers'. This is particularly true in the Paris area. None of the Parisians I know thinks it is in any way odd to summon the fire brigade in the event of a car crash or for someone who has had a heart attack in the street. If there really is a fire, a fire engine turns up when you dial *18*. If, however, it is a medical problem, you get the SAMU, le Service d'Aide Médicale Urgente. This is a fire-engine-red van filled with 'pompiers' who are also paramedics. People refer to the emergency vehicle itself as a SAMU, which is very annoying for the blokes inside for they believe that they are driving a SMUR – Service Mobile d'Urgence et de Réanimation. Calling an ambulance, which you do by dialling 15, is for minor dramas when there is more time available. Indeed, if you call an ambulance for a serious emergency, you will be routed through to the 'pompiers'. By the way, while the French traditionally dislike their police and find them stupid, they absolutely adore their firemen.

Doigts The French are surprisingly organized when it comes to naming their fingers. Each French finger has its own name rather than a vague description as in English, where they are called the ring finger or the middle finger. In French, starting from the one nearest the thumb, you have: 'l'index', 'le majeur' – middle/biggest finger, 'l'annulaire' – ring finger and, last but not least, 'l'auriculaire' – little finger. The word 'auriculaire' comes from the Latin word for ear because the finger in question is the only one small enough to stick in your ear! For the French are great ones for scratching an itchy ear. It seems absurd to generalize about a nation when it relates to something as peculiar as ear-scratching, but I am forced to do so. I imagine that you have never been struck by the way an Englishman scratches an itch in his ear. It is hardly the sort of thing you notice. Any Brit faced with an itch would, I'm sure, try to deal with it as discreetly as possible, probably using the tip of an index finger. In France things are far more spectacular. French men have a particular way of scratching their ears. I have observed lots of men on trains or buses, or passing the time in their car at traffic lights, who insert the tip of their 'auriculaire' as far as it will go into their ear, while keeping the other fingers clenched and the elbow well out to the side. Once the little finger is in place, they will shake it with surprising violence both round and round and in and out for some seconds. Then, with an expression of relief and contentment, the finger is withdrawn.

Écoutez! If you want to be sure of hearing this word, ask a prominent figure a question. The more important the person, the more likely he will begin his reply with *Écoutez!* The word literally means listen, but it is used as a sort of warming-up moment when the person is still marshalling his thoughts before replying but doesn't want anyone else to start talking. It also serves to make sure that the other person is paying attention and is ready for whatever momentous statement is about to come forth. It is very rare indeed to see a politician being interviewed on TV who doesn't answer at least one question with the word. It sometimes appears that the more annoying the politician finds the question, the more he is likely to start with a firm *Écoutez!* If it is said in an aggressive tone, it can almost mean, 'Now you just listen to me . . .' If you know the person well and use 'tu' to them, you will say 'Écoute!' instead of *Écoutez!* My boss uses this to show that he is on familiar terms with someone important. When telling me about a conversation he has had with some such person, he will say, 'So I said to him, "*Écoute*, Pierre . . ."' Unfortunately for him, this fails to impress me in the slightest.

Élections

If you want to follow French presidential elections, even though you can't vote, you will need to learn a few words. First of all, the election usually involves two stages: an elimination round, known as 'le premier tour', and a final contest between the two candidates who received the most votes in the first round known, unsurprisingly, as 'le second tour'. The voting procedure is complex. You need to go to your polling station, often at the local Mairie, clutching your 'carte électorale' or your identity card. Scrupulous checks of the electoral roll are made before you are allowed to go into 'l'isoloir', a voting booth which has a curtain extending down to waist height. On the way to 'l'isoloir' you have to pick up at least two voting slips, each bearing the name of one candidate, because voting is carried out by putting a pre-printed slip of paper in the voting envelope rather than by marking a cross against a name on a list. You are not allowed to take just one slip because this would enable an observer to know whom you have voted for. This rule is taken very seriously and leads to a huge wastage of voting slips, some people picking up one for each of the candidates who, in the first round, can be quite numerous. Having put your voting slip in the envelope, you then leave the booth and head for the ballot box, where your name is checked again. Once all is well, the man will pull a lever to open the slot on the top of the box, watch carefully while you post in your vote, and then declare loudly 'A voté!', whereupon a mark is made against your name. Voting closes at 8 p.m. at which point all the TV channels announce the winner on the basis of detailed exit polls carried out throughout the day.

Exclusion An all-purpose word that concerns the difficult relationship between the haves and the have nots in France. France, like the UK, has its share of homeless people, drug addicts and immigrants, whose future is uncertain. Whenever newspapers refer to the problems of such unfortunates, the word *exclusion* is generally used to cover their common difficulties. These are often related to the fact that those who are better off, who have jobs, a home and a future, not only don't do anything to improve the unlucky ones' lot, they pretend that they don't exist. The fact of being ignored and rejected by society is summed up by 'l'*exclusion*'. Politicians make long impassioned speeches urging action 'contre l'*exclusion*', while charities raise money to 'se battre contre l'*exclusion*', but nothing much seems to change. The homeless, the unemployed and the other have nots are referred to as 'les exclus'.

Bringing 'les exclus' back into society by giving them a job or a home is defined as 'réinsertion'.

fnac Everyone goes to 'la *fnac*'. 'La *fnac*' – pronounced phnack – is a chain of multi-media large shops easily identifiable by its friendly, lower-case white letters. If you want to buy a CD, a book, a BD or any sort of electronic gadget, you start at 'la *fnac*'. When someone mentions that he is looking for a book to buy, he will rarely say that he will have a look in his local 'librairie' or book-shop, but will think first of all of 'la *fnac*'. The shops can be found in every shopping centre and are popular because they carry out tests, somewhat in the manner of those done by *Which?* magazine, and publish useful free reports setting out the advantages and disadvantages of the various wares on sale. It is also a handy place to buy tickets for exhibitions and concerts. However, I doubt whether one French person in ten has any idea where the name *fnac* comes from, though I have never heard anyone comment on what an odd-sounding thing it is. It is, in fact, an acronym for Fédération Nationale d'Achats pour Cadres or National Federation for Management Purchasing. Once the chain started to become famous, it changed its name, in a spirit of democratization, to Fédération Nationale d'Achats, dispensing with the management bit.

HLM Another acronym. The first step to understanding an acro-nym in a foreign language is to realize when you hear it for the first time that it is, in fact, an acronym and not an odd-sounding word. If you hear that someone lives 'dans une ashellem' you can waste considerable time looking for the word in a dictionary. It is only when you understand that you are dealing with an acronym that you can find out that *HLM* is short for 'habitation à loyer modéré' or low-cost housing. It is roughly synonymous with the English term council flat, notably because *HLM* are far more often flats than houses. I have never heard anyone use the full expression: they just say of someone, 'Il habite dans une *HLM*.' In fact, it is more common for people to say 'dans *un HLM*', which is incorrect as the indefinite article has to agree with the real word 'habitation', which is feminine, and not with the letters, which could arguably be considered masculine.

Journaux The people of Britain adore their newspapers; the people of France like theirs considerably less. A simple check of the circulation figures shows this to be true. In Britain, the *Mirror*, the *Sun* and the *Daily Mail* each has a circulation in excess of 2 million copies a day, with the *Daily Express* and the *Daily Telegraph* selling around a million each. That is a lot of newsprint. To the daily papers should be added, at least in London, the *Evening Standard*, which has a circulation of over 400,000. In France, the total number of newspapers sold each day is less than the circulation of the *Sun*. For example, France's major newspaper, *Le Monde*, is the biggest seller but has a circulation of only 400,000. Second comes *Le Figaro*, which sells 370,000 copies a day. *Le Monde* is an odd newspaper. It comes out in the evening but is dated the following morning. Then there is *L'Équipe*, which is the third-best-selling newspaper in France but is by far the most fun to read. It contains all manner of articles but exclusively relating to a single subject, sport. Other newspapers have sports supplements or sports pages, but *L'Équipe* has stories about nothing else.

La Here, we are talking about *la* the musical note, not 'la' the definite article, nor yet 'là' with the accent on the a which means there. The French tonic scale does not go Doh, ray, me, fah, soh, la, ti, doh as Julie Andrews taught us. In France it goes 'Do, ré, mi, fa, sol, *la*, si, do', which must make the French version of the song quite odd. I only mention *la* in this context because of a fascinating fact: the French dialling tone is a perfect *la* or A. This is a handy thing to know if you ever want to tune a musical instrument and have only a telephone to hand.

Nombres

Writing words in French is hard enough for the British because you have to add the accents over and under some of the letters. According to French friends, non-French people do funny accents which are immediately recognizable as the handiwork of a foreigner. It is something to do with starting them from the wrong end. Or possibly, going in the wrong direction.

But worse than accents is the problem of writing figures. For French 1s, 7s and 9s are not like English ones. Of course you know that continental 7s are crossed, but the 9s are odd in that they have tails which curl round more than English ones. And by far the oddest are the handwritten 1s. These have an angled bar at the top which makes them look like a tired and depressed 7. The faster French people write their 1s, the bigger the droopy arm tends to get, so that a badly written 1 can end up looking like a deformed n. There are tales of French doctors writing prescriptions for English tourists which led the poor patient to take 7 pills instead of 1 because of the bad writing. Even though I now cross my 7s, all my numbers still look decidedly un-French.

Numéros de téléphone

In Britain you give out your phone number digit by digit so that you say something like oh, one, five, eight, seven, four ... In France you have to dictate your phone number in pairs, each pair being a two-digit number. This means that you don't say five eight, seven four, but fifty-eight, seventy-four, and so on. Even this wouldn't be a problem if it weren't for the infernal French numbering system. Numbers in French are logical enough as far as they go, which, oddly perhaps, is up to sixty-nine, after which logic goes out of the window. Up to sixty-nine the numbering corresponds to the English way with numbers for twenty, thirty, forty and so on being based on the numbers for two, three and four with a suffix added to show that it is a multiple of ten. You then just attach the required numerals so that the French for forty-two is 'quarante-deux', sixty-five becoming 'soixante-cinq'. All simple so far. Then we come to seventy, which instead of being something logical like 'septante', is in fact 'soixante-dix' or sixty ten. Things get even worse fairly rapidly for, after ploughing through a series of additions including the equivalent of sixty twelve – 'soixante-douze' – and sixty nineteen – 'soixante-dix-neuf' – we reach a new mathematical plateau with the number for eighty. Here addition is abandoned in favour of multiplication and eighty becomes 'quatre-vingts', or four twenties. The long climb up to a hundred includes both multiplication and addition with ninety-three being 'quatre-vingt-treize', or four twenties thirteen, and ninety-nine being the incredible 'quatre-vingt-dix-neuf', or four twenties nineteen. All this may explain why the French are better at arithmetic than the Brits. This peculiar counting method causes problems when a French person gives you their phone number. Whereas with a British phone number you can write down the digits as soon as you hear them, in France you have to wait for the end of each pair. What's more, if the number includes figures beginning with 'soixante' or 'quatre-vingts', you can't start writing before you have heard the whole number. If you hear 'soixante' and immediately write a 6 you may have to change it to a 7 if the number turns out to be 'soixante-douze'. It is all very time consuming.

-O It is time for another wild generalization: the French have a thing about abbreviations that end in *o*. French people like nothing better than shortening a word and there is a whole series of words which, when shortened, end in *o*. Many of these are medical terms and possibly reflect their habit of going to see specialists at the drop of a hat. For example, if you have a skin problem, you go to a dermatologist or 'dermatologue', or, if you are a woman, you may go to a gynaecologist or 'gynécologue'. In either case, when talking about it, the patient would not use the proper word but would say that she had been 'Chez le dermato' or would go 'Voir la gynéco'. If they were regular patients, they would call them '*Ma* dermato' or '*Ma* gynéco'. Away from things medical, abbreviations ending in *o* also crop up in the gym where abdominal exercises, which are properly known as 'exercises abdominaux', are invariably referred to as 'abdos'. This should not be confused with 'ado', which is a common abbreviation of the word 'adolescent'. The habit even extends to the environment, where 'les écologistes' are commonly called 'les écolos', people of the green persuasion being referred to as 'très écolos'.

Primo, secundo, tertio When making a series of points in an argument, the French occasionally start counting in Latin. This is quite surprising when you hear it for the first time. Instead of saying 'premièrement' for firstly, they will prefix their first important point with the word *primo*. In the unlikely event that they don't get interrupted and manage to get to their second and third points, these would be prefixed by *secundo* and *tertio* respectively. However, while people generally start off correctly, they often go wrong later on. The second point often becomes 'deuxio' instead of *secundo*, presumably as a corruption of the word 'deux'.

Sommier This is a word whose existence I had never imagined until the day I went to buy a bed in France. 'Un *sommier*' can best be defined as the bit of the bed you didn't know you had to buy. I have looked it up in a French–English dictionary but there doesn't appear to be a translation for it. It is a word you learn when you are in a state of extreme weakness. You have wandered round a furniture shop, increasingly troubled by the cost of the beds, until you have at last found one that more or less meets your requirements. Of course, you had realized that the mattress would be sold separately, but had foolishly imagined that the price you saw attached to the rest of the bed itself would cover all you needed to buy. Think again because there are in fact two labels attached to the bed. One for a sizeable sum which turns out to cover the bed itself – the bit you can see when you walk into the bedroom – and a second, for a lesser amount, which relates to 'le *sommier*'. This, you at last discover, is the wooden frame that sits inside the bed and holds up the mattress. Why it is sold separately is beyond me. The bed isn't a bed without it because the mattress would end up on the floor. I have never bought a bed in the UK and thus have no idea whether such sneaky behaviour is peculiar to France.

Suppositoire The list of things that might make you stop and think twice about coming to spend some time in France must include 'les *suppositoires*'. (Those of a sensitive disposition should perhaps move quickly on to the next paragraph.) In my sheltered youth, i.e. the part that was spent happily in England, I had never considered suppositories as a serious means of medication. My first encounter with them was when looking through my parents-in-law's bathroom cabinet in search of aspirin. The search revealed a packet, claiming to deal with 'maux de têtes', or headaches, which seemed promising. Opening it, I came upon the most surprising objects that I had ever seen in, or outside, a bathroom. Discreet questions were answered with an alarmingly unambiguous gesture explaining where such products were intended to be inserted. A reply along the lines of 'Good heavens! But I'm English' led to mockery and ridicule. 'Mais, c'est très efficace,' I was assured, but to no avail. I think we should leave this subject here.

And there is no way that I am going to discuss French thermometers, apart from relating the drama in an Oxford prep school where my wife was briefly a matron responsible for the health of a dozen eleven-year-old boys. One poor kid was traumatized for life when, on complaining that he thought he had a temperature, he was pursued around the house by a French girl with a thermometer who demanded that he remove his shorts 'tout de suite'.

Syndic/syndicat Confusion arose because I thought that one of these was the abbreviation of the other. The error came to light when I couldn't understand why our residents' association should be run by a trade union. *Syndicat* is the French word for trade union. The three principal trade unions are all known by their initials: you have FO (Force Ouvrière), CGT (whatever) and CFDT (whatever too), whose representatives regularly appear on news programmes announcing future strikes or justifying previous ones. 'Un *syndic*', on the other hand, is the name for the management committee that runs the day-to-day affairs of an apartment building or other collective dwelling. It is to 'le *syndic*' that you turn when you think the heating should be switched on early, or when you need to find out whether you are allowed to put up a satellite dish, or when you want to complain about your neighbour's dog. 'Le *syndic*' also organizes the annual 'réunion des copropriétaires' as the residents' annual general meeting is known. This is a dreadful affair that lasts for hours and involves voting on topics both important and unimportant. It is the only occasion during the year when older residents can speak at length in public, and also gives residents the opportunity to exact public vengeance on anyone who has caused offence since the last meeting.

Virgule We have encountered all sorts of surprising things relating to French vocabulary, but there are even surprises when it comes to maths. The most astonishing thing is the fact that a simple decimal point is not universal. I happily translated two point five as 'deux point cinq' in the first weeks I lived in France because it never occurred to me that anyone might use anything other than a decimal point. But of course they do. The point between the integer and the decimal fraction is not a point but a comma in France. Thus, French people say 'deux virgule cinq'. This is something that should be taken into account each time you write a cheque because fifteen euros and thirty centimes is 15,30 and not 15.30 (which, in France, is half past three). When you write big numbers in English, like fifteen thousand four hundred and ten, you would write 15,410. The French maintain their way of inverting commas and points by writing 15.410. Thus, a cheque for a large amount would be something like 15.410,65 instead of 15,410.65.

The Business World

So, after reading all the preceding sections, and learning all the words, you must be thinking 'But, how can I get a job in France?' I shall therefore finish with a selection of words covering how to get a job, and all the wonderful things you will discover once you have got it.

GETTING A JOB

Bosser No one actually works in France. By this I mean that no one uses the verb 'travailler' to describe whatever activity they do while at their employer's place of business. This activity is invariably described by the slang verb *bosser*. Using this word manages to imply that the work being done is strenuous, tiring or difficult; doing something nice, that you actually enjoy, would never be defined as '*bosser*'. After a long, tiring week, you might collapse at home with the words 'C'est fou ce que j'ai bossé cette semaine.' Work itself – strictly 'travail' – has its own slang term, which is 'boulot'. This can cover both the job: 'Qu'est-ce que tu fais comme *boulot*?' or the quantity of work you have to do: 'J'ai énormément de *boulot* à faire aujourd'hui.' You can also use *bosser* for intellectual work such as studying for an exam, an activity that could be described as 'Il faut que je bosse mon examen,' while revising your Spanish would be '*bosser* mon espagnol'.

Cedex This is a word that you often see at the end of a business address on an envelope. Not so much when you are writing to a big company or a private firm, but more when you are writing to an organization that expects to receive a lot of post that they need to deal with rapidly. *Cedex* stands for Courrier d'Entreprise à Distribution EXceptionnelle – or special delivery for business letters. In fact, in order to be sure of receiving the letters early in the morning, the company has to fetch them from the post office rather than wait for the postman to deliver them. Experience shows that, just because a company has a *Cedex* address, it is no more likely to reply promptly to your letter than any other company.

Formules de politesse This is the French equivalent of the English yours faithfully or yours sincerely which you put at the end of a formal letter. Unfortunately, whereas two words are perfectly sufficient in English, the French have a positively feudal attitude to finishing letters, preferring to use long-winded and ornate phrases which vary depending on the person being written to. Just to give you an example, in a letter which you would simply end yours faithfully, a Frenchman would be expected to write 'Je vous prie d'agréer, Messieurs, l'assurance de mes sentiments distingués.' This roughly translates as begging the recipient of the letter to accept the assurance of the writer's distinguished feelings. I mean really! Can you imagine asking the man from the electricity company to accept the assurance of your distinguished feelings? Or worse, what he might do if he did? It doesn't stop there. If you are writing to a businessman you know, you would finish your letter with 'Je vous prie de croire, cher Monsieur, à l'assurance de mes salutations distinguées' by which you would be asking him to believe in the assurance of your distinguished salutations. How could you possibly know whether he believed them or not, and would it matter if he did?

When it comes to writing to women, the French become uncharacteristically prudish. Finishing a letter to a woman with any reference to feelings is considered unacceptable, for fear, presumably, of inflaming the poor creature's passions. Therefore, in order to preserve her dignity, one is expected to close a letter to a woman with the words 'Je vous prie d'accepter, Madame, l'expression de mes respectueux hommages.' This is guaranteed not to inflame anyone's passions as you are merely asking her to accept the expression of your respectful homage. This is unlikely to catch on in England or become a successful chat-up line.

Lettre de motivation You can't just write and apply for a job in France. Writing a simple letter, the sort of thing that seems quite acceptable in the UK, something along the lines of: I am writing to apply for the position advertised in the *Oxford Mail* dated . . . would be completely unacceptable in France. You have to write 'une *lettre de motivation*' or your chances of getting an interview will be zero. This is the most sycophantic, hypocritical affair, which has to include phrases like 'Votre annonce a retenu toute mon attention' – your advert had me really gripped (well, something like that) – as well as protestations of overwhelming enthusiasm for the job and the company, not to mention your desire to work for them until retirement, if not beyond. Needless to say, such letters are quite tough to write. There is therefore a strong market for books which set out various standard forms of letter that you can adapt to suit your own situation. Having been on the receiving end, as well as the sending end, of such letters, I view the whole thing as a waste of time. I based my selection of candidates to interview on my wife's graphological analysis of the letters – which is much more reliable.

Piston, copinage There must be some conclusion to be drawn about the way things work in France from the fact that they have two common words for something that requires a whole expression to explain in English. We talk about having friends in high places or knowing someone who can pull strings. The French have the word *piston*. If you aren't good enough to achieve something on your own, you need *piston*. This is the sort of help that comes from knowing someone important or from being the nephew of the managing director. Whoever it is will then exert their influence in your favour and the job, or the promotion, is yours, whether you deserved it or not. Your new colleagues will mutter darkly to each other – with a mixture of contempt and jealousy – that you got the job 'par *piston*' or that you were 'pistonné'. It's quite a relief to be English in France because I don't know anyone remotely useful and so no one can ever accuse me of being 'pistonné', even though there are times when it might have come in useful!

The other word for this kind of help is *copinage*, which tends to refer to help that you get specifically from friends or from those who have been to the same GRANDE ÉCOLE as you.

HAVING GOT THE JOB

Chèques déjeuner These are luncheon vouchers, but not quite like their UK counterparts. This came to light on my first morning in my first French office. A distinguished-looking lady appeared in front of me carrying a small booklet. These, she announced, were *chèques déjeuner*, explaining that there was one for each working day of that month, and that each was for a value of 20 francs. (This was many years ago.) When I enthusiastically stretched out my hand for this unexpected present, she firmly asked me for a cheque for 200 francs. It took a while for me to discover what was going on. In France, spending on meals is considered a joint expense between the employer and the employee with each contributing half the cost. Thus, although each cheque was for a nominal 20 francs, the company paid only 10 francs, the other 10 being paid in advance by the employee. Even at the time, it was very difficult to eat at lunchtime in central Paris for only 20 francs. Where a company has an in-house canteen, the employer still contributes towards the cost of the meal, but this is in the form of subsidies which are invisible to the employee.

Comité d'entreprise

At last something that is much better in France: 'le *comité d'entreprise*' of a large organization is the equivalent of a social club writ large. French employment law states that every company with fifty or more employees must have such a club and specifies that it must receive 1 per cent of the total of the company's salaries as a budget. This means that for a large organization, the *comité d'entreprise* has some fairly serious spending power. What does it do with all this money? It funds all the various clubs and associations that are provided for the employees. It organizes holidays at rates well below cost – so cheap that the queue to sign up usually starts to form very early in the morning. The social club makes block bookings for concerts and plays and then subsidizes part of the cost of the ticket. In some companies, there are sports clubs with tennis courts and swimming pools, the running of which is dealt with, and financed by, the *comité d'entreprise*. In others, they opt for higher subsidies for meals served at the canteen. The advantages for the employees are numerous. The cost to the employer is high, which is why some companies carefully arrange not to go above forty-nine employees. The social clubs of some huge organizations, notably the electricity company EdF, have over fifty employees to handle the social affairs (and the enormous budget) and therefore the social club must have its own mini-social club.

Impôts 'Les *impôts*' is a term which casts a chill into the strongest French heart. It means income tax. The French do not like paying income tax and particularly do not like filling in their tax form each year. This is commonly, and incorrectly, known as 'la déclaration des *impôts*' (it should be called 'la déclaration des revenus' as you declare your earnings not your tax). This pastel-coloured, deceptively friendly-looking form drops through the letterbox each year in mid-April, and you have until the end of May to fill it in and send it back. But, more likely than not, you will join the other taxpayers in one of France's great annual events: sticking your tax form in the letterbox outside the tax building on the last possible day. As no one enjoys filling in their form, everyone leaves it to the very last minute, and then, in order to be sure of it arriving on time, most people drive to the tax centre late in the evening to deliver their envelope by hand. Unfortunately, as everyone has had the same idea, you find yourself stuck in huge traffic jams in the area with other uptight and stressed 'contribuables' – taxpayers – hooting their horns furiously. I usually abandon the car some streets away and walk the last few hundred metres. Once you arrive at the door of the tax building, you are faced with another problem. As so many people have already put their envelopes in the letterbox, it is full to overflowing. Last time this happened I didn't want to leave my envelope sticking out of the letterbox where it might blow away or get pinched, so I pulled out a huge handful of other peoples' envelopes and shoved mine well down inside the box before roughly pushing the others back in. I then walked back to the car worrying that someone else might do the same thing. This year I am going to send my form in by post.

Informatique It is a sign of how long I have been living in France that word processors and PCs appeared since I first arrived. I have thus learned the little I know about using Windows software in French and have become used to saying 'copier coller' long before I could cut and paste. In case you ever have to use a French computer when on holiday, for example in an internet café, a few basic terms might be of use. For a start, the Word tool bar which in the UK reads:

File, Edit, View, Insert, Format, Tool, Table, Window

says on my computer:

Fichier, Édition, Affichage, Insertion, Format, Outils, Tableau, Fenêtre.

A mouse is 'une souris', while a mousepad is 'un tapis de souris'. 'Un clic droit' gives you the choice between 'copier, couper et coller'. And 'un fichier et un dossier' correspond to a file and a folder.

Ordinateur In days gone by, when a brand-new device appeared on French soil, the French government and l'Académie Française insisted that whatever it was be given a French name rather than just adopting the English one. This was intended to preserve the French language. As far as I can see, the only time they really succeeded with this strategy was with computer, which translates as un *ordinateur*. This is a made-up word which was selected in place of the alternative, 'un computeur'. It has slipped into the French vocabulary quite happily. The same cannot be said for another made-up word which was supposed to become the generic name for personal stereos of which the forerunner was the Walkman. The Académie came up with 'un balladeur', but this completely failed to gain popular support and is almost never heard. Everybody calls it 'un Walkman'. Indeed, the only person I know who uses the word 'balladeur' is me, purely out of cussedness. It looks as though the government now seem to have given up the battle to retain French words for things because new terms such as USB, CD and ADSL are used exclusively.

Pont An excellent word in that it relates to days off work. While in the UK bank holidays are invariably on a Monday, corresponding public holidays – of which there are a fair few – in France fall on a specific date rather than on a given day of the week, and each year a public holiday shifts to a new day of the week. Every so often, a public holiday will land on a Tuesday or a Thursday, and this is where things get interesting. The majority of employers, in an attempt to improve employee relations, will give their staff the Monday or the Friday off as an extra holiday so as to bridge the gap, or 'faire le *pont*', between the public holiday and the weekend. As soon as you receive next year's new diary, the first thing you do is check the days of the various public holidays and see how many *ponts* you are going to get. May is a wonderful month for *ponts* as there are three public holidays. In peak years when everything falls perfectly you can have three long weekends. Nowadays, however, more and more companies are insisting that the extra days come out of your holiday entitlement. See RTT and VIADUC.

RTT The French working week is very strictly defined. Many years ago, you had to work thirty-nine hours each week. This was real working hours and didn't include the lunch break. About twenty-five years ago, the working week was reduced to 37.5 hours. This is what I used to work when I first came to France. It meant a 7.5-hour working day. Then, the Socialist government came up with the brilliant idea of reducing still further the number of hours worked on the grounds that this would inspire employers to take on extra employees to do the work that was no longer being done by the existing staff. This was intended to reduce unemployment, though it is not clear that any new jobs were really created. What is clear is that *RTT*, which means 'réduction du temps de travail' changed employees' lives immeasurably. Most companies decided that people should still do the same number of hours' work each week, because there was still the same number of things to do, but that the number of days off each year would be increased. The majority of employees received eleven extra days off a year. Rather than give the days off freely, some employers require at least some of these days to be used for training purposes, and that other days be used to make up long weekends – see PONT. Thus, *RTT* days would take the place of free days off that were previously given generously by the employer. Even allowing for that, there are still quite a few extra days off left. *RTT* has changed holiday traditions in France with people using their days at odd times of the year to make up long weekends for short breaks away.

Treizième mois This is a good term to learn if you work in France because it relates to bonus payments. When you attend a job interview and agree on your annual salary, you could reasonably expect that you should receive one twelfth of your agreed pay each month. In fact, this is seldom the case. Traditionally, your salary is divided into thirteen parts with one thirteenth paid each month and the remaining thirteenth paid as a sort of annual bonus. In many companies, you get the thirteenth part just before Christmas so as to be able to squander it on presents. Other organizations pay half the thirteenth month in July to help with holiday expenses, and the other half in December. Clearly, they are not real bonuses: the extra payment was yours anyway; it has just been saved up for you by your employer. Some companies divide your salary into fourteen or even fifteen parts and pay the extra bits at odd intervals throughout the year. This practice leads to much jealousy among the ill-informed, who are heard to mutter bitterly that so-and-so must be vastly wealthy because he earns fourteen months' pay a year. Clearly, it is your total annual salary that really counts, not the number of fractions that it is paid in. For some reason, my current employer divides my annual salary into twelve and a half parts with the extra half a month being paid in December.

Viaduc We have learned the word PONT, which refers to an extra day off taken between a public holiday and the nearest weekend so as to provide a four-day break. Where the public holiday falls on a Wednesday, some people take off two extra days, either at the beginning or at the end of the week, so as to have a really long break. By extension of the PONT or bridge analogy, this is referred to as 'un *viaduc*'.

AND SOME ACRONYMS TO END ON

ANPE It is not the meaning of this acronym that is important – it stands for Agence Nationale Pour l'Emploi, which is the French equivalent of a Job Centre – it is just an example of the numerous

French acronyms which start with an A but somehow sound as though they don't. The problem arises because, in practice, people say l'*ANPE* not *ANPE*. This means that you hear someone say that he is going for an appointment with the words 'Je vais à l'*ANPE*.' This, to the untutored ear, sounds just like saying 'Je vais à la NPE.' If you haven't heard of the *ANPE* you may be fooled into looking up something called NPE which, of course, doesn't exist. This is probably not deliberate trickery on the part of the French, but one can never be sure.

Similarly, unemployment benefit is called 'l'Assedic' which, when you hear it for the first time, can fool you into thinking that you are dealing with the non-existent 'la Cédic.'

CAC 40 Pronounced 'cack quarante', the *CAC 40* is the French equivalent of the FTSE share index. It stands for 'Cotation Assistée en Continu' and comprises, as the name suggests, the share prices of the top forty French companies. As with other share indices, the CAC's health is widely reported, often in medical terms. When the economy is doing well, 'le CAC se porte très bien.' Conversely, when shares are falling, 'le CAC a passé une très mauvaise journée.' The Parisian stock exchange is known as la Bourse and is housed in an imposing building called le Palais Brongniart, which sits in Place de la Bourse in the 2ème 'arrondissement'. Incidentally, the top Parisian restaurants keep an eye on the CAC because they tend to have more customers when the index is rising.

Sigle 'Un *sigle*' is an acronym – a set of letters that is used instead of a series of words. French acronyms aren't always as difficult as they first appear if you use the try-the-letters-another-way-round strategy. If faced with TVA, you may not have any idea what it might stand for. But if you try the letters another way round, you get VAT. If the words are generally similar, only the order will change as the adjectives are put after the subject. Thus, Value Added Tax is 'Taxe à Valeur Ajoutée'. Similarly, while you might not recognize SIDA, changing the letters around gives AIDS, which is much more familiar. It doesn't always work, of course. The World Health Organisation is l'Organisation Mondiale de la Santé. Do what you will with OMS, you won't end up with WHO. Nevertheless, rather than giving up in despair at the sight of a French acronym, changing the letters round is often worth a try. Here's an easy one to start with! Have a go with the international organization known in France as l'OTAN.

Smic Another acronym which is used as a noun. There is a strictly defined and regulated minimum wage in France and it is known as 'le *Smic*'. This means 'le Salaire Minimum Interprofessionnel de Croissance'. It was created by law on 2 January 1970 and replaced something called 'le Smig' or 'le Salaire Minimum Interprofessionnel Garanti'. Interestingly, thirty-five years on, people still pronounce it 'Smig' rather than *Smic*. When talking about jobs, notably for young people on courses, they will say 'Il va toucher le *Smic*' or 'Il va être payé au *Smic*.' Even though most people don't know what the *Smic* currently is to the nearest euro per hour, they know it isn't much and that being paid it is not a good thing. Poor unfortunates who earn the *Smic* for life are known as 'Smicards'. The amount of the *Smic* is revised in line with inflation each July and currently stands at €8.03 per hour or €1,217 per month.

Index

-Marie 123
-o 206

À cheval 15
À jeun 90
À poil 158
Adjectif 45
Aïe! *see* Paf, pan, plouf
Ancien combattant 148
Anglais 145
Angleterre 145
ANPE 224
Apéro 5
Appel de phares 31
Arheu 188
Arme blanche 195
Assedic *see* ANPE
Atmosphère 69
Au plaisir! 177
Auld Alliance 147

Bac 53
Badaboum! *see* Paf, pan, plouf
Bagnole *see* Flotte, flotter
Baguette 11
Baise-en-ville 182

Baiser 182
Banane *see* Pêche
BCBG 177
BD 158
Bic 195
Bière 5
Bilingue 136
Bis 196
Bise 183
Bison Futé 31
Bizarre 69
Bon appétit! 178
Bon . . ., Bonne . . . 179
Bonjour, m'ssieurs,
    dames 179
Bonne continuation 178
Bonne fête 100
Bordel 159
Bosser 215
Bouffer 15
Boulangerie/pâtisserie 12
Boulot *see* Bosser
Boum *see* Fête, boum, soirée,
    teuf
Brave 113
Bye-bye 137

CAC 40 225
Caca *see* Pipi, caca
Café gourmand 16
Câlin 184
Canard 6
Carnet 38
Carte d'identité 83
Carte de séjour 83
Carte orange 38
Cartes de vœux 102
Cassoulet *see* Couscous,
    cassoulet, choucroute,
    confit
Cedex 215
Certain 113
Chambre/Salon 114
Champagne 7
Chants des supporteurs 72
Châtaignes *see* Marrons
Chèques déjeuner 218
Chéquier 90
Cheval 73
Chez 114
Chiffres 196
Chiottes 159
Chocolatine *see* Pain au
    chocolat/chocolatine
Choucroute *see* Couscous,
    cassoulet, choucroute,
    confit

Choutte 160
Circulez! 32
Classe préparatoire 59
Clope 161
Clous 33
Coca 7
Cocorico 73
Coef *see* Coefficient
Coefficient 54
Comité d'entreprise 219
Composter 29
Con 161
Condamné 115
Confit *see* Couscous, cassoulet,
    choucroute, confit
Consommation 34
Constat 34
Contrepèterie 162
Copain, copine 185
Copinage *see* Piston, copinage
Copine *see* Copain, copine
Coup 8
Coup de cœur 197
Couscous, cassoulet,
    choucroute, confit 16
Couvent/couvent 115
Crème anglaise 18
Cucul 116
Cuisson 18
Cyclistes 73

D'accord 116
De 117
Début 137
Dégriffé 197
Deux . . . deux 8
18 (dix-huit) 198
Dodo 162
Doigts 199
DOM-TOM 40
Donner du sang 91
Dont/que 117

Eau 19
Eau de source 9
Écoutez! 199
Élections 200
En revanche 118
Énarque *see* Gadzart
Espace 118
Et avec ceci? 12
Étoile 42
Étrennes 103
Exclusion 201

Fanfare 74
Fête, boum, soirée, teuf 186
Feux 35
Fille, meuf, nana 157
Flotte, flotter 163
Flotter *see* Flotte

fnac 202
Foi *see* Foie/foi/fois/Foix
Foie/foi/fois/Foix 119
Fois *see* Foie/foi/fois/Foix
Foix *see* Foie/foi/fois/Foix
Fonctionnaire 84
Formule 20
Formules de politesse 216
Franglais 137
Frites *see* Pêche

Gadzart 60
Galette 20
Gare! 119
Gars *see* Mec, gars, type
Gâteau 13
Génial! 163
Gentil 120
Glace sans tain 121
Grandes Écoles 61

H 121
Haro 122
Hexagone 41
HLM 202

Impossible 85
Impôts 220
Informatique 221
Ingénieur 63

Intellectuel 63
Invariable 122

Jeanne d'Arc 148
Jour férié 101
Journaux 203

L'Argus 91
L'ennemi héréditaire 146
La 203
La Chandeleur 21
'La Marseillaise' 150
La petite see Le petit, la petite
La rentrée 55
Le petit, la petite 188
Les Belges 147
Les bleus 75
Les filles!, Les garçons! 157
Les garçons! see Les filles!, Les
    garçons!
Lettre de motivation 217
Lettre recommandée 92
Lieu de naissance 86
Livret A 93
Livret de famille 87

Machin see Truc
Maghreb 41
Mamie see Pépé, Mémé, Papy,
    Mamie

Manger chaud 22
Marguerite see Médor
Marianne 93
Marignan 1515 149
Marques d'affection 186
Marrons 22
Maths sup, maths spé 61
Mec, gars, type 157
Médor 70
Mémé see Pépé, Mémé, Papy,
    Mamie
Mercredi 101
Merde! 164
'Messieurs les Anglais, tirez
    les premiers!' 146
Meuf see Fille, meuf, nana
Midi/le Midi 99
Mince! 164
Minou see Médor
Monsieur 23
Moquette see Tapis
Morceau de sucre 138

Nana see Fille, meuf, nana
Navarre 151
Neuf trois 42
Noël 104
Nom de famille 86
Nombres 204
Non! 151

Nous 75
Nul 164
Numéros de téléphone
  204

Oh la la! 165
On 124
Ordinateur 221
Ouais 166
Oui 88
Ouistiti! 46
Ouvreuse 70

Paf, pan, plouf 125
Pain 24
Pain au chocolat/
  chocolatine 14
Pan see Paf, pan, plouf
Pantomime 71
Papy see Pépé, Mémé, Papy,
  Mamie
Paquet cadeau 104
Pardon? 180
Parigot 42
Pas évident 126
Patate see Pêche
Pâtisserie see Boulangerie/
  pâtisserie
Pavillon 126
Pêche 24

Pépé, Mémé, Papy,
  Mamie 189
Perfide Albion 146
Périph see Périphérique
Périphérique 44
Perpète les Oies 47
Péter 127
Petit 127
Philo see Philosophie
Philosophie 56
Photographe 128
Pièce montée 89
Pièces jaunes 106
Pipi, caca 189
Piston, copinage 217
Plouf see Paf, pan, plouf
Poc see Paf, pan, plouf
Poire see Pêche
Pom Pom see Médor
Pomme see Pêche
Pont 222
Pot 9
Pote 166
Pourboire 10
Prépa see Classe préparatoire
Primo, secundo, tertio 206
Priorité à droite 35
Punaise/purée 167
Purée see Punaise/purée
PV 36

Qu'à cela ne tienne 129
Que *see* Dont/que
Quoi . . . ? 167

Radio 129
RATP, RER, SNCF 40
Re- 180
RER *see* RATP, RER, SNCF
Réveillon 105
Rhume 130
Rigoler 168
Rond point 37
Royaume Uni 147
RTT 222

Sac en plastique 187
Salon *see* Chambre/Salon
Salut! 181
Sandwich 25
Scotch 130
SDF 94
Sécher 56
Secundo *see* Primo, secundo, tertio
Seizième 44
Service National 64
Si/si 131
Sigle 225
Signes du zodiaque 107
Smic 226

SNCF *see* RATP, RER, SNCF
Soireé *see* Fête, boum, soirée, teuf
Soleil 57
Sommier 207
Sports 76
Subjonctif 131
Suppositoire 207
Sympa 168
Syndic/syndicat 208
Syndicat *see* Syndic/syndicat
Système D. 132

Ta gueule! 169
Table des matières 57
Tablette de chocolat 25
Tapis 132
Tartine 14
Télévision 72
Tertio *see* Primo, secundo, tertio
Teuf *see* Fête, boum, soirée, teuf
Théme *see* Version
Tiercé 76
Tiret 58
Toussaint 105
Treizième mois 223
Trente-trois 133

Trifouillis les Oies *see* Perpète
   les Oies
Troisième mi-temps 77
Trou Normand 26
Truc 169
Tutoyer 133
Tuyau 133
Type *see* Mec, gars, type

Vachement 170
Vélo 77
Verge 48
Verlan 170
Version 134

Viaduc 224
20 (vingt) 59
Virages 78
Virgule 209
Vivement 134
Vlan *see* Paf, pan, plouf
VO/VF 138
Voie 135
Vouvoyer 135

X 62

Zef *see* Flotte, flotter
Zinc 10